faith over all

JAMIN ANNE HART

WOODSONG
PUBLISHING

Faith Over All

Jamin Anne Hart

ISBN 979-8-9855200-2-6

Cover Design by Jeremy Hart for Hart Creative + Design

Published by Woodsong Publishing
Seymour, IN

Printed in United States of America.

Dedicated to

my Grandma, Rebekah Reece

who has continually chosen faith over all.

contents

a tale of three couches

I never did grow up completely. As if carrying "fishy crackers" in my purse for myself wasn't a tell-tale sign alone, I came to this revelation when the new and supposed "put-together-evangelist wife" found herself in a snow ball fight with a thirteen year old pastor's son. There I was, like a child, picking up the powdered Missouri fresh snowfall with my bare hands, yelling out competitive threats, and feeling a bit too much at home. I threw that snowball with all my might, only to watch in horror as the snowball missed the tall thirteen year old, and in midair did a unique one hundred and sixty degree turn, just in time to explode on the introverted pastor's back. I was mortified. Our precious evangelism ministry flashed before my eyes.

After haunting seconds of silence, to my shock and utmost relief, the pastor erupted in laughter and wiped away the snow saying, "That was a good one, that was a good one." A good one, indeed! I worried that we would never be booked for another revival when this got out! Now, how we laugh every time we reminisce about that afternoon.

I am not a polished, put together or perfect evangelist wife. I am passionate, loud, exciting, competitive, and emotional with many unnecessary tears. Come to find out, God created us not to hold fancy titles: He created us to be ourselves and within that, a faithful servant for Him.

CHILDLIKE FAITH

A child has nothing but hope and dreams for his future, unaffected by the temperaments of life. The definition of faith is "the substance of things hoped for." So, like every other girl, I hoped for the man of my dreams. And oh, how I had faith it would happen! I had heard enough love stories from the missionaries and evangelists who had come through our church and home, and I desired their kind of relationship. To me, there is nothing more beautiful than a love story with Jesus at the center of it all. Two lives given to working together in the Kingdom of God, surely that is the greatest love story of all time! That is why it is a mystery to me how I could forget the nine words I had written down in an old journal at the age of seventeen.

Somehow in the shuffle of life, the clear voice of God that evening was put away from my memory. That is, until I started dating Jeremy. One day, when the engagement was drawing near, I reminiscently began to read through an old journal and there I rediscovered those nine words: "Tonight, God called me to be an evangelist wife."

I suddenly remembered the night vividly. It was an autumn evening during a weekend revival at my home church in Moose Lake, Minnesota. I had taken my place in the back corner of the sanctuary where I loved to pray. I longed to see more of God, desperate to know what He desired for my life. Loving his presence above this present world and knowing that life was

10

most beautiful when it is lived for Him, I desired Jesus to be with me every step of the way. I desired big things. I had big dreams. I couldn't be content with ordinary things. I knew that in my momentary loneliness, God saw the forever companionship of my future soulmate. I knew God is the ultimate author of our stories, and He knows the end even in our beginning. Holding the worn journal, I sat back in my couch. That is why it had never felt right with anyone else! God had created me with Jeremy Hart in mind and had already put in place a plan, all those years ago, for our paths to come together. Oh how we cheapen ourselves when we say we want a love story like the movies. God writes love stories much better than any Hollywood producer. As we see evidence in creation, so we see the evidence of God's detail oriented attention to our lives in such a way that leaves us astounded at the thought of such divine love and care.

Script writers write because of their great imagination or educated ability, but God is the origin of every creative thought and source of every human ability; therefore, how much better a story might He be able to write? Besides, God's specialty is love. In fact, God is love. To write our own story, to attempt to replicate the fanciful story of someone else, will only end with shattered disappointment and pain. When we allow God to continually write our story, the ending is always the best part because He saves the very best for last.

MARRYING THE EVANGELIST

To share my story of this season of life, being an evangelist wife and sharing the Gospel, I must begin by telling how I came to marry the evangelist. It is my favorite story to share, and yet, the hardest to write, for the things closest to our hearts are often the most difficult to put from pen to paper. It is as if simple words strung together do an injustice when compared to the romantic beauty of the reality we ourselves lived. At least, this is how I feel when trying to tell our love story. Yet still I share, merely hoping it will come across as wonderful as it first happened.

Jeremy and I first met at a dinner table after church on the final night of General Conference in Indianapolis, Indiana. The restaurant was swarmed with peers and fellow students from Indiana Bible College, where I was attending and in my senior year. Our mutual friend, Mark, had invited him along and saved him a seat, that is until someone with a crush on Mark sat down and refused to get up. The only other available seat was at my table across from me and my friends. Mark told us someone was coming, but I had never met him. Jeremy soon arrived and, once seated, the introductions were made. He told our friend sitting next to him that he was on a low carb diet, which I did not hear. So when Jeremy asked the table, "What's the best thing on the menu?" I immediately piped up, feeling quite extroverted in front of this quiet newcomer, and I informed him that the very best entrée was the deep-fried mac and cheese and pulled pork sandwich. Oops. I hadn't heard him say anything about a diet, so the first words spoken to me by Jeremy Hart, outside of "Hello, it's great to meet you," were "Yeah, I'm not gonna get that."

Well, then! I lifted my little eyebrows and looked at my friend Samantha sitting next to me as if to say, "He's all yours." How we laugh about that now. The conversation moved on, and we didn't say much of anything else to each other throughout the course of dinner, and I left with some friends soon after finishing my meal. A couple months later, my friend Samantha brought up Jeremy's name in conversation. I had heard his music playing in her dorm room before, which was funny enough in itself because this northern girl was not raised on southern gospel. I had heard enough of Samantha and his conversations to catch a glimpse of his character and kindness and, although I don't know where it came from, I looked at her and said, "He is my ideal type." Those words surprised me more than they did my friends. Even with our not so romantic exchange of food suggestion and rejection, I just knew there was something about him. His life was clearly kingdom minded and his heart was settled. I felt like I knew him, even though we had hardly shared more than a few words. His spirit and character had shown brighter than his quiet words. And let's be real, to any wild extrovert, an introvert is very enchanting. But this was beyond some clever use of the word enchanting; God had his hand upon it. I knew he was everything I ever wanted and would be content to be with him forever. Samantha didn't waste time breaking the news of my new love interest to the one person who could bring Jeremy and me together. Mark immediately sent Jeremy a text message, asking if he remembered meeting Jamin Reece in that crowded restaurant on the Friday evening of General Conference. Jeremy remembered, and Mark, unbeknown to me, quickly told Jeremy all about me and sent a YouTube video of me singing Still Gonna Praise You on the Indiana Bible College live recording. Jeremy still was only a distant, almost unrealistic, thought in my mind, never knowing God and Mark were at work.

A Tale of Three Couches

THE FIRST COUCH

One specific day in January, I really began to pray about my future husband. Daily I would pray in my dorm room, kneeling at my well-worn and fringed old couch. It was not fringed by design nor for looks; rather, it was fringed from unraveling and falling apart in its old age.

On my knees, I began to tell God how much I desired a man who would seek Him with his whole heart, who would pray and be willing to kneel next to me, and us seek the face of God together. I was weeping. I do that a lot. I am emotional. Yet God knew the desire in my heart and right then, the Lord spoke to me: Jeremy Hart will. Jeremy will be on his knees seeking my face next to you. It was more of an overwhelming thought than an audible voice, but it was real. The sheer shock of such clarity was almost overwhelming. Jeremy had not even reached out to me yet. Besides our brief encounter at dinner in early October, three months before, we had not exchanged one word, and yet it was so clear. So clear in fact, I jumped up from my room and ran to my friend's dorm room to excitedly share what I felt. "I can't explain it, but Jeremy Hart is the one for me! I think I'm going to marry him!" She laughed and laughed, proclaiming that he wasn't my type, his music wasn't my style, and that we wouldn't even look good together. Of course, she also included that we didn't even know each other! I was embarrassed and quickly retreated, never speaking another word about it. I learned instantly that some God moments are meant to be kept between just you and God. Sometimes the deep moments with Him, what we feel and what we hear Him say are not meant to

14

be shared with others until God brings all things into alignment and fulfills what He has promised.

While this was happening in Indiana, Jeremy was at a conference in Alexandria, Louisiana. While God spoke to me, He also spoke to Jeremy and assured him that the timing was now right and He was about to answer one of his greatest prayers. Jeremy had not had a girlfriend or been in a serious relationship since he started evangelizing, which had at that time been five years. His ministry was everything to Him. Eight hundred and sixteen miles from the worn-out couch where God has spoken to me, God impressed upon Jeremy's heart that it was me, Jamin Anne, he should pursue. God gave him an overwhelming peace, and on February first, he messaged me on social media.

I had never experienced conversations with anyone like I did with him, then, and even now. There has always been a part of my heart that I could never share with any other man for fear he would think I was silly, or wouldn't understand me for who I really was, until I met Jeremy. I would find myself anxiously looking forward to any chance in between classes or after work when I could message him back an equally long response as what he had sent me. My friends affectionately called them "books," but there was so much to talk about: music, his songwriting, his travels, what evangelizing was really like behind the scenes. Almost immediately I saw how kind, helpful, and interesting he was. When he asked me to send him a recording of a song I had written, he said I would have to text it to him because it probably wouldn't go through social media. It was sneaky, but that is how he got my number, and we began to text. The afternoon of our first phone conversation, I sat a nervous and

15

excited wreck in my car holding tight to my phone until the call came through. And then, so I didn't look too eager, answered it on the third ring. His voice was more southern and slow than I had remembered. I found it quite attractive and soon this northern girl began quickly babbling the thing closest to my heart: ministry. It seemed that was the common theme within our hearts. Within the next month, he told me that as soon as his ministry schedule made the time available, he was going to come visit me at Indiana Bible College.

It was the first week of April when he arrived and, strangely enough, one of my busiest weeks of the semester. I will never forget seeing him walk from the shadows of the parking lot to the brightly lit sidewalk steps, just outside of the student lobby entrance, where I was waiting for him. He was wearing light colored jeans and a grey vest. Instantly I decided I liked his casual style. I decided I liked him a lot.

The next day after classes were dismissed and work was over, I went back to my dorm room where I carefully picked out a teal blue blouse and navy sweater to wear on our first date. We decided to eat at a local pizza favorite, and soon my phone alerted me that he had arrived at the school and was waiting for me at the iconic place where all the college guys pickup and drop-off their dates. I had walked down the steps into the student lobby a thousand times before, but never was I so excited and anxious as when I looked through the glass and saw him. Feeling confident in my blue, we said hello and walked together out to the curb where his shiny Honda CR-V was waiting. It looked like a Porsche compared to my little Chevrolet Impala LS. He opened my door, and I remember mumbling "I love your car," which I soon regretted because he probably thought I was crazy. We proceeded to talk effortlessly all the way across Indianapolis to the restaurant. It seemed he knew about everything! I couldn't stop asking him questions. I have never had a problem finding things to say, yet with him, it seemed I only wanted to hear what he had to say. When we had finished our meal, he said the dreamy words, "Do you want dessert?" If he knew the answer to the question would be yes for the rest of his life, he might not have asked; but he did, and gleefully I accepted his offer. Within minutes, we were sharing a cookie skillet.

When our first date was over and I had been dropped off at the school, I anxiously ran to my dorm room and called my mom to tell her, "I'm going to marry him, mom!" Somehow she wasn't surprised. Although she had not yet met Jeremy, she and my dad felt I would marry him. When Jeremy got back to where he was staying, he called his best friend in Oklahoma and said, "Unless something crazy happens, I'm going to marry this girl." He was godly in conversation and character. He was so kind and such a gentleman that I found myself overwhelmingly drawn to him. He was balanced, yet he was far from boring! He was confident with pure humility. I had never been myself around someone to this level. I truly felt like we were made of the same soul.

The next day he heard me speak in the Tuesday morning college chapel service. Two days later, he picked me up from work to drive me to Bloomington, Indiana, where I was leading worship for a revival. When he saw me coming out of work, he jumped out to open my door and accompanying him was a gorgeous bouquet of brightly colorful flowers and my favorite chocolate bars. Inside his car, a Subway sandwich was waiting for me since I hadn't had time to eat that day. My heart was soaring higher than a hot air balloon, higher than the stars. I had never felt so taken care of as he drove me to the revival service.

After leading worship that night, I came down from the platform and sat next to him on the second row. Everything about that night felt right. The way he took care of me, our conversations, and now, being together in a ministry setting made my heart burst. After eating dinner with the pastor, we headed down the road toward Indianapolis and, both knowing he was leaving the next morning, were keenly aware nothing had been said about our feelings. He had never flirted in our conversations, he had never said, "I like you." He had never even indicated that he thought I was beautiful. However, it didn't take him long after leaving the restaurant in Bloomington for him to break the silence and tell me his feelings. In his southern voice, he began carefully, yet with confidence. He told me how seriously he took his ministry, how he had decided not to date until he knew it was right, and yet how he felt such peace about our relationship. I couldn't help but grin from ear to ear when he said he had never met anyone like me. He then proceeded to tell me he knew it would be long distance due to his travels, but he committed to do whatever it took to make it work. I couldn't contain or hold back the smile that was bursting on my face, and that smile hasn't stopped since. By the end of the drive, I mustered up the courage to ask him, still hardly believing this was real, "Does this mean I can call you my boyfriend?" He looked at me and replied at the corner of East Sumner Avenue, "Only if I have the honor of calling you my girlfriend." I didn't sleep much that night. Reality was much better than my dreams.

The next morning before he left, we went to my favorite brunch spot. Before we said our goodbyes, he reached over and took my hand for the very first time. With sincerity I had never seen before, he said, "You are absolutely gorgeous." It was the first time he had told me I was beautiful. All I could do was whisper, "Thank you," as my face clearly reflected a thrilling, but overwhelming, state of shock.

One month later, Jeremy came back to Indianapolis to attend my graduation and celebrate my birthday. The day before graduation, we walked the canals of downtown Indianapolis hand in hand. As the rain began to fall on us, we paused, and despite the storm above, he held my hands, looked me in the eyes, and there he first told me he loved me. Maybe that is what made it all more perfect—to know first in a storm, he loves me.

THE SECOND COUCH

Within eight months, we were married on a cold December night in a winter wonderland wedding, where we were sent off into married life on the back of a vintage snowmobile and matching sleigh, our friends and family waving sparklers that glistened off the fresh snowfall. After our honeymoon on Minnesota's beautiful north shore, we began full-time RV life on the road, evangelizing together and loving the life God had given us together.

Within a short few weeks of marriage, we were preaching at a wonderful church in a small southern Arkansas town, staying in their evangelist quarters. In my purse I had brought a bag of my favorite chocolates and placed them in a glass bowl on the table. My favorite coffee beans were placed next to the coffee pot to make it feel a little bit like home. I hung up my dresses in the closet, almost giddy for the services in which I would be testifying and singing next to my brand new husband and hearing him preach each night. I was anxious to spend time with the pastor's family; they had two teenagers. I love connecting with pastors' kids because I remember being a pastor's kid and looking forward to the moments an evangelist couple would come to our church and take time to make me feel special.

I glanced around, taking everything in like a sponge, even the picture on the walls. One painting was of a mother and daughter in white dresses, both with long sandy blonde hair, that capture the epitome of just how beautiful holiness unto God is. On another wall there hung a large painting of an old pioneer preacher baptizing a soul in a cold river. My heart was exploding from the overwhelming emotion of peace and joy I found in living for Jesus, and soon I found my place at the end of the couch in the living room where I went to my knees in prayer.

After a few moments of prayer, I looked over and saw Jeremy kneeling on the other end of the couch, seeking the face of God. It was only then that I remembered the word's God had spoken to my heart one year before, as I knelt at my worn out tattered couch in the Indiana Bible College dorm room: Jeremy Hart will. Jeremy will be on his knees seeking my face next to you.

Sometime after our third wedding anniversary, we were visiting a Bible college, and a student approached me, asking how Jeremy came into my life. The words popped out before I hardly realized what I was saying. "I prayed him into my life." It then dawned on me just how true that statement was. There were many moments I would go into the prayer room on the girls dorm floor at Indiana Bible College and when others were hanging out, I would hang out with Jesus. Of course, I did my share of socializing and networking among friends, for I am an extrovert after all, but I couldn't be myself without time spent with the Lord. He knew all of my desires. He knew how badly I longed for a companion to share in all my adventures, a romance that was pure, someone with the same convictions I held in my heart, the same interests, a man who would sweep me off my feet with chocolate and flowers, a home filled with godly conversations and peaceful evenings where I would cook and we would laugh. I wanted a man who would let me be me and love me for it, a man who loved truth and ministry. I not only told myself these things, I told God also.

If you earnestly desire something, pray about it. The common denominator of everything good, pure, and wonderful in my life is a result of prayer. I sought the face of God, I poured my heart out to God, and preparing me in His timing, He gave me the desires of my heart. Only God can take our lives and write masterpieces. When God writes the story, there will always be details of priceless significance that neither you nor I could ever bring to fruition.

There is no such thing as a perfect person, a perfect family, or perfect marriage, but there are perfect gifts we can obtain from above. God gives us perfect gifts. When those gifts are wrapped within our marriage, family, or spouse, it is far more beautiful than any story fabricated by the entertainment industry, because it is divinely designed by the Lord. Jeremy is my gift from God. As it happens, a certain magic kingdom is really not where dreams come true. It is the Kingdom of God!

21

A Tale of Three Couches

THE THIRD COUCH

In all of our sightseeing and adventures, nothing compares to the joy I feel in my heart when Jeremy and I wake up, make our pot of black coffee, and spend time in prayer and in the Word of God together. It is a taste of heaven found within marriage.

I have found my identity and dreams begin nestled in those moments of prayer at this couch. I think of the beauty that came of moments knelt at the tattered couch through my college days. I think of the moments in the evangelist quarters, hotels, kneeling on their couches. The prayers that have been answered go beyond what we can see in the natural.

This third couch is my place in my home where I find Jesus. It is where I call on His name to tell him of my fears, my worries, my desperation, my thankfulness, my needs, my hunger and desire. It is this third couch where I am living in now, my altar, where the half will never be told. A place of prayer is where I find my strength. I understand how John could pen the words, "And there are also many other things which Jesus did, which, if they should be written every one, I suppose that even the world itself could not contain the books that should be written" (John 21:25).

To write everything that our Savior has done in my own life, my pen would soon run out of ink. Some prayers are so intimate; I cannot write them down for eyes to gaze upon. The miraculous that has taken place in my mind time and again, it is too personal to share with mere words. I think of the moments where I have found God within my tears, as they have seeped into the leather couch in the motorhome, hearing the groans and desires of my heart. I understand why the psalmist wrote in "I am weary with my groaning; all the night make I my bed to swim; I water my couch with my tears" (Psalm 6:6).

Prayers for my husband, for my family, for the young people in my life that I believe in more than they know. Personal prayers, desperate prayers, selfish prayers, unselfish prayers. Prayers for our nation, prayers for my world. Prayers for pastor's children, and our own future children. Prayers that contain forgiveness, prayers that include laughter. It is these moments of prayer where I find the strength to be selfless, and the audacity to whisper the words, I give you my life, Jesus. Where you lead me, I will go.

A COUCH IN THE ROYAL PALACE

Sometimes I wonder how Esther managed to have such grace and courage. I am not at all comparing my own story to hers, nor my strength to her strength. My own selflessness often wavers and is only found again through prayer. Yet her story proves an unending truth of where to find these qualities: it is always prayer. There is a layer within a life living for God that remains the same, for I know her strength was found in her devotion to the one true God whom she served.

Serving, cooking, and cleaning was her life in a humble home. Worn and dirtied clothes was what she was accustomed to, yet she was lovely, positive, and of an encouraging spirit. I imagine in her home with cousin Mordicai, she had a place where she would pour her heart out to God. Maybe it was kneeling at her humble excuse for furniture, her couch, on the dirt floor. She was both Jew and slave, trapped in the bonds of exile, yet before those titles, a child of God.

With a turn of political events and one decree from the king's court summoning all fair virgins, she found herself in the royal palace a part of the most memorable beauty competition that we still speak of all these centuries later. What a change for Esther! She had seven personal attendants, her own hairstylist, dress designers, six month beauty treatments of myrrh proceeded by six months of perfumes and ointment treatment. There was plenty portions of divine food she did not have to prepare, brought on platters of gold, filled with the best fruits and breads in the land. Far from the simplicity of her life with her cousin, even the most gracious heart is not exempt from feeling the overwhelming emotional pressure. I can imagine Esther having moments of fear, doubt, and many tears. It was against her own wishes after all, that she was thrown into a foreign atmosphere of riches and glamour in every direction. Yet her walk with God never wavered.

From poverty to a palace, it is hard to wrap our minds around the grandeur in which she then lived. The garden alone was beautifully decorated of hangings of white and blue linen, fastened with cords of white linen and purple material to silver rings on marble pillars (Esther 1:6 NIV). And as the Bible describes all the wonderful beauty she herself was encompassed with, we are also given one more detail that I could hardly believe! Something else was mentioned within the palace. "There were couches of gold and silver on a mosaic pavement of marble, mother-of-pearl, and other costly stones" ((Esther 1:6 NIV).

A couch. A place to kneel. Oh my, perhaps her place of prayer. New surroundings do not suddenly change who we are and our character. For surely it was not her outward beauty alone that won the heart of the King: it was her inward purity and humble character. Esther's identity was in God. Her place of prayer in the palace may have looked different, but it was the same relationship. Our daily habits and emotions do not dissipate by new locations and adornments. Whether we are dressed in rags on riches, we feel the same pain and emotion alike. The truth is, it doesn't matter your surroundings, it only matters your connection. Strength does not automatically come with a crown, it comes with relationship. Purpose, fulfillment, and joy do not come with marriage as some magical packaged deal, it comes through prayer and character alone. Titles do not change us; rather, daily habits change us. Soon, by divine orchestration and position, she became queen of the royal palace.

I can picture Esther, in all of her royal garments and costly array, kneeling down on the cold marble. What a dynamic contrast to the dirt floor she used to kneel upon to pray. Perhaps she, too, thought back to those moments at her worn couch in her old home, yet it was the same voice in prayer once again.

Within prayer is found the unique and exclusive invitation for God to ordain our steps, even when it entails plans beyond our understanding. It is only after time with God she found the strength to rise up and declare the courageous words, "... and if I perish, I perish" (Esther 4:16). Time in His presence exposes the heart of God: Others, people, freedom. There was no selfishness within enjoying the grandeur alone for Esther, for riches are often empty without others. It was and will always be first and foremost about the Kingdom of God, and all else shall be added unto you. Prayer is where we see the beginning of the miraculous, and the courage to stand if it does not come to pass. And yet for Esther, it did come to pass, and through the favor of God and man, her people were set free.

A Tale of Three Couches

Strength and joy are not handed to us; there is a daily walk with God that uncovers those gifts. We can easily fall into the trap to look at another's life, admire their strength, joy, and accomplishments. But hidden behind them is hard work and daily choices that do not always come easily.

I look back at the epoch moments in my life. Although all are in different locations and surroundings, one thing remained: I had an altar. It was certainly not a replica of the altar in the Old Testament Tabernacle. Its wood was not rare. It had no shine or shimmer. In fact, the cushions were flattening, the fabric fading and frayed, but it was my altar. I had a relationship with Jesus, and within that creates a tale greater than a fable, it is a life story that comes alive and anchored in prayer. What a blessing it is to watch God bring to pass desires and purpose in our life greater than ever imagined.

CHAPTER TWO

fourteen

days

There was not as much adjustment as might be expected to full-time RV living, full-time evangelizing, and being a newly wedded wife. The only home we had known together was our thirty-seven foot motorhome with three slide outs, and before long I had decorated every nook and cranny. Bless my husband's heart. Being from Moose Lake, Minnesota, I really kept the northern theme alive. Actually, I think he liked it and even added his own deer antlers to the decor. It felt like our own little northern resort on wheels, even garnished with candy dishes and the ever present aroma of coffee brewing in the pot. Married life was just beginning, and I had fallen in love not only with him but our home on wheels.

Most of the time we park and set up the RV in the parking lot of whatever church we are preaching at, but the occasions we park at a scenic campground are always an exciting experience. Trying local coffee shops and restaurants make every small town or big city feel welcoming. The constant meeting of new people as we walk into new churches makes the extrovert in me come alive! Right away I noticed there are many cultures, decor styles, and personalities within each church, and yet there is spirit and truth in each one. However new the church or unfamiliar the people were to me, I have found myself right at home and overwhelmed with the presence of God that we feel there. One cannot help but grow in faith when you see first hand, from state to state, Jesus heal sick bodies and fill hungry, repentant hearts with His Spirit. God is no respecter of persons and, in both big churches and small churches alike, I have yet to find a way to articulate how each church has built my faith.

Ultimately, I am left overwhelmingly grateful each time I walk onto a platform to sing songs written from my very own heart, with my husband, never taking for granted the realization that God has far surpassed my wildest dreams. It certainly has its challenges, but I am unspeakably thankful that God called me to this wonderful life and gave me both the passion and personality for constant travel, ministering to people, and enjoying such an adventurous lifestyle.

OLD PAIN AND A NEW PROMISE

Right in the midst of the unspeakable joy of those first few months of evangelizing and marriage, a previous neck and back injury decided to flare up. And boy, do I mean flare up!
Remember when my husband first told me he loved me in a rain storm? Three months into marriage, we were about to face far more than a romantic downpour.

I must have lifted something I shouldn't have. I don't have any idea what caused it, but I remember well the pain I experienced during a particular Wednesday night service. We were preaching in Oklahoma. The motorhome was parked just outside the side door of the sanctuary, and I remember praying that God would help me make it through my husband's message before collapsing into the motorhome. Somehow I did make it through, and as soon as church was over, I told Jeremy how I was feeling. I wanted to crawl in bed and somehow fall asleep, yet that seemed so utterly impossible due to the intense migraine headache and throbbing neck pain I was suffering. We told the pastor and his wife, who were gracious and full of understanding. Before Jeremy and I slipped out the side door of the sanctuary, they prayed with me. Every time I think of that service, more than the pain, I remember their prayers over me.

The night was long and morning eventually came, but holding no promise of relief, we decided to check out a local chiropractor. I had been to chiropractors multiple times before with nothing ever going wrong, yet that day broke the clean record. There was something very wrong. This lady claimed to be an experienced professional but did the exact opposite of everything we asked her to do. Just after we had carefully explained in detail the inflammation and injury to my low back, she laid me on the table, bent my knee and pushed my leg up toward my chest, and not gently. With all of her strength and body weight, she threw herself down onto my bent leg and proceeded to adjust my lower back three consecutive times. She then proceeded to tell me that I would be sore because of all her "adjusting." My husband, who had never been to a chiropractor, was horrified. The whole scenario would have been extremely humorous if it had not have been so painful.

We left the chiropractor's office and drove to Oklahoma City for a conference we had planned to attend. I tolerated the pain that evening during church, but by the next morning it was intensifying. I tried to be strong because I didn't want to look weak in front of my brand new husband. Throughout the night and early Friday morning, I began to complain of the pain, and he sweetly reminded me that the chiropractor said I would be sore and encouraged me to take something to help the pain. I complied and took some Advil. Jeremy went to a minister's business meeting, and I went to a coffee shop with a friend. That was when the pain in my back escalated to a whole new level of unbearable. Sitting with a friend, I suddenly felt light headed and began fighting to remain conscious due to the dynamic duo of pain and fear. I just wanted Jeremy. I wanted the comfort and kindness of my husband. I was scared. My friend rushed me back to Jeremy, who left his meeting and took me to an urgent care. They gave me muscle relaxers and said there wasn't much they could do until the inflammation went down. That night, although I was in pain, I did not want to miss the church service at our district conference. As soon as the worship began, I felt better. I suppose it is natural, but I have the tendency to get overwhelmingly fearful when I know something isn't right in my body. But in the presence of God that night, I felt safe and at home. Every fear was chased away. This is why His glory, the fullness of His presence, is something I pray everyone experiences.

As worship broke forth in the room of several hundred believers, I felt a woman I did not know put her hand on my back and pray with me. She then spoke in my ear, "God is the one bringing you through what you are going through right now. It is to bring you closer to God and to your husband." It was all I needed to know: God sees me! Of course, the logical part of me knew God always sees me, but my heart was assured in that moment. God sent someone who had no idea what I was facing to let me know everything would be okay. At the same time, another minister approached Jeremy, who was praying next to me, and told him almost the same thing that had been spoken to me.

On the way back to the motorhome that night I told my husband, "That is why we go to church." To leave a service feeling refreshed, encouraged, and filled with direction is why we gather and why God shows up among us. Jeremy and I shared our hearts and talked over everything we had heard and felt during that night's service. I love those moments with him, sharing our hearts and talking about the goodness of God. I was filled with the encouragement that is found in the house of God.

The Sunday following the conference, I was only able to attend one of the two services we had scheduled and spent the majority of that service in the pastor's office because the pain was sickening. My husband expressed to me that evening how hard it was for him to preach when he knew I was in the pastor's office in pain. We then scheduled an MRI on my lower back because I was convinced that such intense pain had to be more than inflammation alone. Even though it would bring answers, I dreaded the MRI. It almost screams, "Something is wrong with you" when one is in the tube. But I was thankful for the Christian music they let me listen to, and you better believe I prayed the whole time I was in there. The enemy was trying to speak through fear, but I was determined to silence those voices with my voice lifted in prayer to God.

After the MRI had been completed, my husband took me to eat and told me to get any piece of cheesecake I desired. Funny. Now I realize it isn't the uncomfortableness of the MRI machine I remember from that day, it is how I felt when I held the to-go box of cheesecake on my lap in the car while Jeremy held my other hand.

It was then that Jeremy and I recalled a spontaneous statement he had made a few weeks earlier while he was preaching. "I can go through anything if I have a word from God," he had said. As soon as the words left his lips, he paused. He had to keep preaching but immediately knew that somehow that statement would be challenged and we would have to personally experience the test. That statement had been forgotten until several days into my pain. Thanks a lot, my dear husband!

After four nights with no sleep, partly due to the steroid shot and partly to the pain, and after two more trips to the emergency room, I was surprised when the MRI results showed that my pain was only inflammation and muscle spasms. I had a hard time believing something so simple could cause so much pain. There were many nights my husband would sit up with me because muscle relaxers and pain medicine did not touch it. He would hold me, and I would remember the sweet promise from the Lord. Truly, it was He who was taking us through this to be drawn closer together. It hurt, but I knew that if God is involved, I would be okay.

Pain exposes true character. As for my husband, I already knew his impeccable character, yet I grew all the more thankful for this kind and loving man whom God had given me. Pain has a way of bringing people together. There is a level of closeness that is only possible to experience by way of brokenness and pain. It is in our weakness where God desires to show His true love to us. When we feel a failure and are unable to give in our weakness, that is the very place in which he delights to show Himself strong.

Within those fourteen days, and after a second trip to the emergency room for them confirming only time will take care of the inflammation and my pain, we attempted the trip to Minnesota that we had scheduled months prior. We were to preach a Wednesday evening service in Des Moines, Iowa, but that morning's hospital visit delayed our leaving long enough that we were unable to make it to church. Nevertheless, we pointed our Honda toward Minnesota. We got as far as Ames, Iowa, when I became sick again. We ended up stopping at another urgent care to get some relief from the pain. After waiting for three hours, a doctor finally came in and offered me a muscle relaxer shot that might bring some relief. I accepted, and unfortunately got up too quickly after being given this shot. Barely making it to the waiting room, I fainted. My lips turned purple, and my face became pale. It is a terrible place to be, half conscience, calling Jeremy's name, not seeing anything. It was not a good day for me. I was scared, and I stuck close to my husband who never left my side.

After leaving the hospital, we decided to forego that day's traveling plans and stay an extra day in Iowa so that I could get to bed and rest up. Although those were painful days that I do not want to relive, I will never forget the closeness of my husband and my God. In fact, I better understand now why Scriptures likens God's love for the church to the love of a husband toward his wife. Jeremy made sure I had comfort, help, and everything I needed or could possibly want. I rested and the next day was able to travel the remaining five hours to Minnesota.

Even though there are equally twenty-four hours in a day, why does it seem the good pass quickly and the hard days drag on? It had been fourteen days since the pain began. I woke up in Minnesota on the fifteen day to find the pain had nearly vanished, the inflammation had faded, and the muscles had ceased their violent and visible spasms. Fourteen days in a storm and finally, on

35

the fifteenth day, it gave way to sunshine and a new appreciation for the precious Word of God.

In the whole scope of hardship, it was as short as a finger snap. Perhaps it seems silly when compared to the trials of others, yet its impact on me changed me. Although a trial be short lived, the effects last forever. The one truth that those fourteen days left marked upon my heart is this: I can make it though the storm with a Word from the Lord. That is not to say we neglect prayer, negate the hardship or are excused from sacrifice, yet we will stand on the other side of a storm according to our faith in God's promise.

I am thankful for the one night in the midst of those fourteen days where I went to church and received a Word from God.

More than two years later, while writing this chapter and simultaneously studying the Book of Acts in my morning devotion, a passage of Scripture caught my eye like a burning flame in a dark night. It was a passage I can relate to, right down to the number of days. I do not pretend to have been in as cold or gruesome of a storm as Paul, but I know what having a promise through pain feels like, as did he.

PAUL'S FOURTEEN DAYS

In the midst of Paul's incredible ministry, there came unto him a new unforeseen circumstance in Acts 23. What started with harsh accusations toward him in the Sanhedrin led him to another dirty dungeon for simply preaching Jesus. On the stone cold floor and in the darkness of the underbelly of the castle, Paul must have felt fear. The crowds of hopeful distractions were gone, the preaching opportunities seemed to fade, and in his chilling loneliness, the foreboding reality sank in: this could be the end. Isolation and loneliness have a way of exposing our deepest insecurities. His mind surely raced as he recited in his mind every sentence spoken in the council of the Sanhedrin, and found fault in his own words. Yet God's timing is perfect. It was in these emotions of loneliness, self doubt, and frustration of failures that grew with the dampening surroundings, "The Lord stood by him." Isn't it amazing that when we think we have found a place where God cannot see us, in that very place he is willing to appear unto us and show His strength. He is not limited to moving only in the company of crowds, but He will come visit us in the solitude of our loneliness.

"And the night following the Lord stood by him, and said, Be of good cheer, Paul: for as thou hast testified of me in Jerusalem, so must thou bear witness also at Rome."
Acts 23:11

Oh my! A word so bright it surely lit up the prison cell with the radiant glory of God's divine assurance. Paul had received not only a promise of more ministry to come but also a hope of fruitfulness in his future. If God said he would bear witness at Rome, to be sure, no one or no thing could keep him from fulfilling what God had promised. Undoubtedly, the mission would be accomplished! Oh how Paul must have willingly let hot tears run down his face as his soul was surely warmed by the presence of the Almighty. Truly, it is not our surroundings that command our outcome but a relationship with the One who controls every outcome. Yet receiving a word from God does not mean it will be smooth sailing from then on out.

Fourteen Days

In fact, before Paul ever reached sea and his ship met a storm, he endured much pain.

How many times had the promise appeared to be in jeopardy? A murderous plot of the oath bound Jews, the delaying of Felix which led to two years in prison, and the attempted compromise of Festus were each the efforts of the adversary to nullify the promise of God and prevent Paul's arrival at Rome. All having failed, a new danger appeared that threatened Paul's promise. Now on the treacherous voyage to Rome aboard a ship with a two hundred and sixty seven member crew, they found themselves caught in the vicious throws of a raging storm. These waves were not the gentle, relaxing kind made perfect for sunshine and a fruit smoothie. These were the angry kind that violently threaten everything in their reach. The waves and gusts of the gale forced their course in a direction opposite of their intention. Paul warned them:

> Men, I can see that our voyage is going to be disastrous and bring great loss to ship and cargo, and to our own lives also. But the centurion, instead of listening to what Paul said, followed the advice of the pilot and of the owner of the ship. Since the harbor was unsuitable to winter in, the majority decided that we should sail on, hoping to reach Phoenix and winter there.
> Acts 27:10-12 (NIV)

The fury of both wind and wave made it necessary to secure and lighten the ship. Ropes were carefully run underneath the vessel to sturdy it's fragile state and hold it together. Much like in the story of Jonah, cargo and tackle were thrown overboard into the angry water.

When neither sun nor stars appeared for many days and the storm continued raging, we finally gave up all hope of being saved.
Acts 27:20 (NIV)

When the desperate and hungered passengers were about to give up, Paul interrupted their starvation and discouragement.

Paul urged them all to eat. "For the last fourteen days," he said, "you have been in constant suspense and have gone without food — you haven't eaten anything. Now I urge you to take some food. You need it to survive. Not one of you will lose a single hair from his head." After he said this, he took some bread and gave thanks to God in front of them all. Then he broke it and began to eat. They were all encouraged and ate some food themselves.
Acts 27:33-36 (NIV)

The only one who had not surrendered to the hopelessness at hand and maintained an unclouded mind was Paul, the man with a Word from God. Faith in God's Word is the sustainer and source of all hope. They had ignored Paul's earlier advice, yet this time found strength and encouragement in his words and took action in eating at the sound of a promised future. Against all seeming reality, they would live and not die.

On the fourteenth night we were still being driven across the Adriatic[c] Sea, when about midnight the sailors sensed they were approaching land.
Acts 27:27 (NIV)

Fourteen Days

Fourteen days! Paul had been in his storm for fourteen days before seeing any promise of shore. It was on the fifteenth day, when out of obedience to Paul, everyone aboard ship put sandal to shore and safely breathed a sigh of relief.

The centurion...ordered those who could swim to jump overboard first and get to land. The rest were to get there on planks or on other pieces of the ship. In this way everyone reached land safely.
Acts 27:43-44 (NIV)

What a traumatic two weeks those were, even for Paul. With the promise from God packed away in his heart, Paul suffered the storm, endured the tempest and survived the angry sea. God's Word did not keep Paul from the storm, it kept him in the storm until it passed. The fifteenth day brought them to the island of Malta where they found a fire of warmth and revival. Remember those spontaneous, God-inspired words that snuck their way into my husband's sermon? "I can go through anything if I have a Word from God." Oh, how true it is, and with so much more confidence can I add my voice to his. With God's Word, we can make it through any storm.

Storms change us. They teach the truth that God hasn't brought us this far to leave us. Paul, although having faith at sea, stepped onto that island with greater faith. No, he hadn't arrived at the place of God's promising, but he was another step closer. Therefore, no weapon formed against him could prosper. The venomous viper that came out of the firewood was nothing for Paul to fear. If God could keep him in the strength of the storm, God would also keep him from the sting of the snake.

The final fifteen verses of the book of Acts tell of Paul preaching Jesus in Rome. Though bound to his dwelling and held under Roman guard, Paul had peace in knowing that he had reached the place of God's intention and thus determined to carry out the divine purpose for his Roman arrival. He preached Jesus.

He proclaimed the kingdom of God and taught about the Lord Jesus
Christ—with all boldness and without hindrance!
Acts 28:31 (NIV)

Paul not only preached to them, but his witness and testimony still speaks to us. My storm wasn't literal like Paul's, nor was I near unto death as he and the ship's crew; however, hopefully, between the two of us, I have articulated to you the truth that with a Word from God you can make it! When circumstances scream "It's over," God's Word quietly proves its infallibility and faithfulness. God says "No, it's not over. I've just begun." And with a Word from God, I can make it.

Should I ever have to walk through fourteen days of pain again, I have the comfort of knowing that it will be fourteen days spent with His hand in mine and His Word in my heart.

For all the promises of God in him are yea, and in him Amen, unto
the glory of God by us.
2 Corinthians 1:20

41

Fourteen Days

But they that wait upon the LORD shall renew their strength; they shall mount up with wings as eagles; they shall run, and not be weary; and they shall walk, and not faint.
Isaiah 40:31

CHAPTER THREE

beginning at bozeman

"Well, you look nice," called our friendly, RV neighbors from their lawn chairs. They were in the campsite across from ours at the campground in Coeur d'Alene, Idaho. It was the evening of my birthday, and we were headed to do a Friday night community concert at the church we had been in revival with that week. I had opened the RV door and confidently made my way down the steps, feeling much like a princess in my brand new blue and white birthday dress, white high-heeled shoes, and countless, multiple curls framing my face. How could I blame them for noticing my dressy attire in a dirt covered campground? The last several days they had seen me walking the campground roads in an oversized T-shirt, work out skirt, and pony tail hidden under my baseball cap. Clearly, the contrast was stark, and I now looked much different than the girl they had seen exercising in a skirt. Yet, it wasn't their words that were noteworthy, it was my response. "Yep!" I proclaimed, "I'm all scrubbed up!" Nervously chuckling, they each nodded as my husband then descended the steps of the RV behind me in his suit. Waving to the couple, Jeremy wished them a relaxing evening, and we let ourselves into our car. No sooner than I sat down, I miserably said, "Jeremy, please tell me I did not just tell those people, 'I'm all scrubbed up.'" Oh, I had. I had, and

45

my husband wasn't even surprised. In his words, "Nothing really surprises me anymore."

I was horrified. Now, contemplating my words, I made it sound like my bathing and cleaning up was a strange and unusual occasion. In fact, I made it sound as though I was proud of myself for taking a bath! Welcome to our life, where amid the constant travel in our motorhome as we minister together all over the United States, there is never a dull moment. To fully appreciate this joyous birthday evening, I must recount for you the journey that brought us to that memorable night.

MIRACLES AMID THE NORTHWEST

There is a genuine, beside-myself type of excitement I feel when our preaching schedule leads to somewhere new. On this particular six-week trip to the northwest, our thirty-seven feet of RV, plus thirteen feet of tow car, was traveling from Muskogee, Oklahoma, to Spokane, Washington. The front half of that route isn't too exciting, but the back half is beautifully scenic with quaint mountain towns along the way. I enjoy traveling in the motorhome the best, not only because I can sleep in the bedroom while Jeremy drives, or make a pot of coffee with my favorite beans as the highway blurs by, but I can see everything through the windshield. It almost feels like I'm out there in the middle of the scenery. The first two days of that trip were long, hard days of constant driving. By the end of day two, we rolled into Bozeman, Montana, where Jeremy had made a campground reservation. After nearly fifteen hundred miles, we needed a couple of days to rest and enjoy the mountainous view. Bozeman, Montana! Big Sky, Montana! These were places that I only dreamed of going when I was a child. I never dared imagined it would be in a RV, heading to preach and sing with my husband over weeks of revivals out in one of the most beautiful parts of our country. God was exceeding my dreams, and my joyful, exploding heart could not deny it.

After we settled into our campsite, we made some coffee, sat outside in the chilly April mountain air, and planned our sight-seeing schedule for the next day. The beauty of Big Sky did not disappoint the next day with its crystal clear streams, majestic mountain passes, and open sky, nor did the town of Bozeman disappoint with their scattered coffee roasters, tourist shops selling overpriced Patagonia hiking gear, and my beloved tourist postcards. There is a certain feeling within mountain towns, and I love it. Casual. Adventurous. Everyone is there together to see the same beautiful surroundings.

We spent a wonderful two days there, but as the sight seeing days came to an end, we arrived back at our campground to find an extraordinarily large problem. Our motorhome was coming apart. The bolts that fastened the outside wall to the floor frame, above the driver's side tire and in front of the driver's seat, had been ripped out of their threads and created a gap. Essentially, the first two feet of our front driver's side wall had detached from the frame.

Suddenly the joy of the mountain peak views fell flat in light of our new found concern. At the end of the day we are not full-time tourists, although that is an occasional added benefit. We are full-time evangelists. We sing, preach, and share the Gospel of Jesus Christ from place to place. Suddenly we realized that our ability to safely travel the interstate, especially through mountains, had come to a screeching halt. It was Friday night, and we had one day to get from Bozeman, Montana, to Spokane, Washington, where we were scheduled to minister on Sunday. We had planned for an easy six or seven hour drive on that Saturday, to be followed by a relaxing evening in Spokane to prepare for revival on Sunday, yet suddenly nothing was going as we planned. Our RV was not in drivable condition. We knew no one to help us in this tourist town. It was eight o'clock on a Friday evening, which meant that any and all RV service centers were closing for the day and quite possibly the entire weekend. Thirdly, my husband didn't know the first place to start in fixing such a perplexing problem. It is one thing to preach that the all-seeing God sees and is attentive to our lives when we feel overwhelmed and deal with discouragement yet it is another thing to live it yourself.

I had heard my husband countless times stand behind pulpits and encourage hearts with Scriptures of comfort declaring what the Psalmist wrote, "The eyes of the Lord are upon the righteous, and his ears are open unto their cry" (Psalm 34:15). We believed that but felt completely overwhelmed and at the end of ourselves.

There we were in Bozeman, Montana, stuck. Jeremy saw only one plan of action. He would have to fix it. Jeremy can do a lot of things, but he would be the first to tell you that he is not a mechanic or auto body repairman. After calling a couple of people and picking their brains, he had a plan that he thought might work but would need the right parts. We jumped up and ran from hardware store to hardware store trying to find a way that we could repair the problem ourselves and get on the road as soon as possible. It wasn't an ideal evening, but it was life.

We had six weeks of revivals scheduled throughout the Northwest and suddenly all of the strength and rest that we had acquired over our two days in Bozeman left, and we felt like we would go into this season of revival, if we ever got there, more exhausted than rejuvenated. Not one store had what my husband needed to fix the issue on the RV. Feeling completely defeated, we held hands in the car and sought the face of God. In almost three and a half years of marriage, I had never seen my husband so discouraged and overwhelmed. Hungry, emotional, and unsure of what to do next, we went to a local fried chicken restaurant to place a take out order. Who cares about calories in a moment like this!

Later, my husband told me that as he stood in the restaurant waiting for our food, he said to himself, "Lord, it sure would be nice if you would lay us on someone's heart and prompt them to call or send a text message of encouragement and assure us that everything is going to be okay." Isn't that what we desire at the end of the day? To know and be reminded that even in the middle of nowhere, without friends, family, or "Mr. Fix-it" to call on, we are not alone, to be assured that we are seen by God!

As we waited for our chicken, my phone dinged. I came alive when I read it. It was from my cousin. She said she was praying for us and was burdened for us, saying "God sees you and is in control." Oh my, the God ordained timing! How thankful I am for sensitive hearts, praying people, timely words more precious than gold, and members of God's body who minister strength to those who are weakened and burdened by life.

The RV still wasn't fixed, but we felt better and stronger with the reassurance that God was with us. We went to bed that night feeling uncertain of tomorrow's journey but encouraged, deciding Jeremy would go to one more parts store early in the morning and believing, in Jesus' Name, the right part would be there, and God would help him fix our RV. In miraculous fashion, God did all that we asked Him to do. By noon the next day, our RV wall was once again fastened and secured in place. God helped Jeremy to fix it. Timing is sometimes funny. The day before, just hours before we noticed the RV issue, I had ordered a half-dozen peanut-butter, frosted donuts from a local hole-in-the-wall shop in Bozeman for the next day. It just so happened that we picked up those donuts before leaving town and had them to enjoy, along with a pot of black coffee, as we pull out of town, thanking God for His help, provision, and guidance. With a donut in one hand and black coffee in the other, I enjoyed the scenic mountainous view from my seat behind the windshield as Jeremy drove.

The trip was going well until, not forty-five minutes down the road, a lady in a red Jeep suddenly appeared in the lane next to us, frantically honking and pointing behind the motorhome. Confused and unsure what could be the problem, Jeremy slowed down and pulled all fifty-feet of our RV and tow car onto the shoulder of the interstate. He and I both hurried outside to see what the problem was, only to find the front driver's side tire on our car completely separated from the wheel. The tread was held only by shreds of the tire that had wrapped around the axle. At this point, we knew that the events of the last twelve hours beyond the shrug of "life happens." We knew that the enemy did not want us in the northwest and was opposing the six weeks of revival that were to begin the next day.

Jeremy dug out a floor jack that had never been used but packed away in one of our under-storage bays, removed the blown tire, and put on the donut spare, while I stood watch and told him when an eighteen wheeler wouldn't get over into the inside lane and come barreling by at a high speed too close for comfort. I felt very helpful! When the job was finished, we cautiously continued our drive through the mountains at a much slower speed, so we didn't risk blowing the donut that probably wasn't rated to travel the distance we needed to go. Our flesh was a little nervous to continue on with the way things were going, and the peanut-butter frosted donuts were a little less appealing now, yet we were determined to get to Spokane. We had only been back on the road a couple of short minutes when Jeremy's phone dinged. A man from southeast Texas, who we'd met during a revival just a few weeks prior, had sent Jeremy a text message that said, "I was in my shop and you came to my mind. I am praying for you guys. Be blessed and know that He has everything under control."

There are no words to describe what that meant to us and the deep appreciation I have for those who are sensitive to the voice of God. Having been on the receiving end of such encouragement and strength, I now seek to be sensitive and more spiritually awake so that I am available should God desire to use me to encourage others in their moments of trial. How often does God seek to get our attention for the purpose of ministering to others, yet our minds are consumed with so many things that seek for our attention? We miss out on so much from the Lord and undoubtedly miss opportunities to be used by Him because of the business of life and the distractions that so easily beset us. Sadly, we even feel justified in our distractions sometimes, yet I challenge us to be more spiritually aware and sensitive to His voice and Spirit.

We slowly continued on our way through the Montana mountains with much caution and concern but with thankful hearts. Somehow the majestic sights outside the window were even more beautiful just knowing that the One who created them had, that very day, shown himself bigger to us than all of the mountains put together.

When we pulled into the KOA Campground, we were delighted and a bit surprised to see our campsite. The church had upgraded our reservation to one of the nicest patio sites with a beautiful wooden swing and brick fire pit. We were scheduled to be parked there for several days and to be in such a relaxing atmosphere, after such a crazy twenty-four hours, was a true blessing from the Lord. When we arrived at church the next morning, we were so incredibly happy to be there after all we had been through and were so refreshed by being in the house of God. I had never met these people or been to this city, and yet it was like being reunited with family. It was not coincidence that their first worship song that morning was "This Means War." (Written by Charles and Tara Jenkins, 2013) Jeremy and I made eye contact from across the sanctuary and our tears said it all. The devil sure had tried to hinder what God had called us to do, but as the song so adequately says, "You can't have my breakthrough. This means war!" After church, I discovered that there was an amazing coffee shop in their foyer that used coffee beans from a local coffee roaster. I sipped on an iced latte while meeting friendly faces and selling our books and music. I turned around when I saw a kind-eyed woman approach me. She looked at me with tears in her eyes saying, "Oh, I'm going to cry!" That was her greeting to me. She slipped me an envelope with my name jotted across it. "I want you to know during church the Lord spoke to my heart and told me to give you all the cash I had in my wallet." With teary eyes and a voice taken away by emotion, she shrugged and said, "It isn't much, but what can I say? This is your money from Jesus." We hugged and teared up together. No matter where we are, I am continually amazed at the body of Christ. I am home when I walk into an Apostolic church!

As if that wasn't enough to be thankful for, Jeremy told me something that I could hardly believe. A man in the church had been outside after service and seen the donut on our car and told Jeremy that he wanted to buy four new tires for our vehicle. You can't tell me God is not real! You'll never convince me that He doesn't take care of His own. God supplied our every need and so much more. What the enemy meant for evil, God turned into good. In our efforts to be a blessing, God blessed us in return. God never ceases to show himself mighty to me. I don't deserve it. I am unworthy. In fact, it is hard for me at times to accept all of the added blessings that God pours out upon my life as I, by His grace, live in the overflow of His goodness and mercy.

That following week was restful as we did a four night revival in Lewiston, Idaho. We were recuperated from the taxing trip we had experienced. Nothing else went wrong and nothing else broke until we arrived in Coeur d'Alene, Idaho. On our first morning at the country fairgrounds campground, we awakened and realized that our water pump had gone out and the shower drain was clogged. The broken water pump wasn't an emergency situation, being that we were hooked up to city water at the campsite. The standing water in the shower floor was, in fact, though. It wasn't a matter of pouring liquid plumber down the drain, something was wrong. It appeared that the problem was somewhere between the p-trap and the grey water tank, so Jeremy began removing access panels to locate the pipe. It appeared that the drain pipe followed the foot of the exterior wall in our bathroom, underneath an L shaped, carpeted cover that hides all kinds of wiring, hoses, and water lines. Jeremy began removing the screws that held that cover in place only to, on the last screw, suddenly smell propane and hear the sound of an air leak. That screw, thought to have been driven into the RV floor, had actually been driven completely through the rubber propane line that fueled our furnace. We were stunned. While Jeremy held his fingers over the two holes in the hose, I ran outside and closed the valve on our onboard propane tank. I had never seen my husband so overwhelmed. It perhaps sounds trivial to a plumber or professional repairmen, but we did not know what to do. We had trouble tracking the hose and were not sure how to get it out. Let's not forget that the shower is still clogged, and we have to get a plumbing snake to run down the pipe. YouTube is an invaluable source of information for RVer's looking to troubleshoot and make repairs on their rigs. Many of the things that service centers charge big bucks to do, some RVer on YouTube can show you how to do yourself. Unfortunately, Jeremy didn't have the tools to do anything else with the drain and couldn't find any helpful information on repairing the propane line. Finally, we left the RV and went to a local place for dinner. We prayed that the Lord would help us, just as He'd done in Bozeman, while we caught our breath over dinner. About the time our number was called and we sat down with our fish and chips, Jeremy received a text message from the Pastor we were beginning revival services with the next evening. He was kindly checking in on us to see if we had settled into the campground and needed anything. Boy, did we need anything! Jeremy briefly told him what was going on and asked if he had a small plumbing snake. The response quickly came back, "Yes I do. I used to work on RV's as a mobile repairmen, as well as for a propane company. Let me know when you're finishing eating, and I will come right over."

I was in awe of God once again. In this specific revival, this specific pastor knew how to fix this specific problem. Coincidence? Not at all. We knew it was Jesus making himself known unto us. We returned to the RV and, while waiting on the pastor to arrive, Jeremy decided to remove the p-trap under the shower and stick a coat hanger down the line to see if he could pull anything out. Sure enough! Out came the most disgusting clod of so many things that should not be clumped together and hanging out in a shower drain. The Pastor pulled up just in time to see it for himself. We were so happy to have one problem solved. Pastor Davis looked at the propane line inside and said, "It's an absolute miracle that you've lived in here for three and half years with a screw through that line and never smelled propane." It was a miracle we were okay. All this time we were living underneath the protection of God, having no idea what all He was protecting us from. I should have been dead, but He's been better than good to me.

It reminded me of a prayer I prayed a couple of years earlier. I had asked God to show me something he had protected me from. I believed I would see it, be it in a vision, a dream, or an impression from the Lord. I did not know how God would answer my prayer, but I believed He would. God loves when we ask bold things. I expected God to show me a car wreck that should have happened or something of that sort, yet weeks later I had a dream one night in which I felt rejection so strong that it was worse than any physical pain. I woke up and ran to my husband. I didn't leave his side all day. I couldn't shake the feeling and urge of just wanting to cling to him, the feeling of the dream still lingering. It was late that evening before falling asleep that I realized the significance of the dream. I knew without a doubt what I had felt was God showing me what he had protected me from experiencing. We never know so many of the things that God protects us from. I just know He deserves our highest praise not only for the things we know He has done but for all those things He has done that we know not of. Sometimes we are inconvenienced by the problems life puts us face to face with and yet, when God is involved we always, in time, see His purpose amid our problems.

It was a special revival in many ways, including being able to spend my birthday with the pastor's family, sightsee in one of most beautiful areas you'll ever see, and minister all the while. Coeur d'Alene has quickly become one of my favorite cities. The day of my birthday, the pastor and his wife came with us to lunch and took us to get dessert at the famous Coeur d'Alene resort, overlooking the beautiful lake and timber covered mountains. Afterward, Jeremy and I walked the world's largest floating boardwalk underneath blue skies and surrounded by teal water. Of all the places I could think to spend my birthday evening, none could be better than being in the house of the Lord. My heart was overjoyed when I saw two visitors walk through the doors, whom we had met the day before while out seeing the town. More kept coming, and soon we counted eleven visitors that had shown up. Who cared about birthday dresses in a moment like this! To see souls who have never experienced a church where there is Spirit and Truth is something more exciting to me than any physical possession or material thing. Good thing! While I was worshiping during our first set of songs, the heel of my white high-heeled shoe broke off, and I had to act natural for the rest of the concert. I watched many of those visitors lift their hands in wonder and worship as they felt the presence of God. From wherever we come and whatever story we tell, the goodness of God's presence draws each of us in. I am continually left standing in awe of how God can mentally, physically, spiritually, and emotionally heal in a matter of mere moments when we are in His presence. That is the greatest birthday gift, the gifts that come from above.

Beyond the beauty of the sights we had taken in that afternoon was the beauty of hungry souls responding to the love of God. He is real! He has not lost His power, He is the same today, yesterday, and forever. I am humbled to be a part of moments like this across the United States.

The enemy had tried so blatantly to discourage and distract us, yet every week, in every city, in every church, and in every revival service God wrought victory after victory.

I learned a lesson over the course of those six weeks: The journey itself takes faith. We expect miracles at the end. We expect excitement upon arrival at the destination. I have no doubt when we walk into churches each week that anything is possible, that miracles signs and wonders can take place when Jesus shows up, yet I never want to forget that when God walks with us and talks with us on a daily basis, there will always be miracles along the way as well. How comforting to know that wherever God is, we are safe! That is why I want Him to fill our home, our vehicles, our marriage, our vacations, our ministry trips. When we walk with Him, we rest in the assurance He goes before us, beside us, and behind us. Of course, that requires something of us. What God can do is most often dependent on what we are willing to do. You and I must be willing to crucify our fleshly human nature each day through repentance and prayer. We must pledge our allegiance to Him and His Word. We must decide that although we live in this world, we will not live according to this world. By giving myself to Him, I am given full access to Him, His presence, and His amazing grace. We must grant unto God full access into our lives, examining every secret area of heart, mind, and soul. The world would call that an invasion of privacy, but how can I keep anything from a God who knows all things about me and formed me from dust?

We know well the miraculous outcome of the three Hebrew boys being thrown into the fiery furnace, but we so easily overlook that it was equally as much a miracle that they even made it into that furnace. The miracle at their destination was the results of a miracle on the journey. Scripture says that "the flames of the fire slew those men that took up Shadrach, Meshach, and Abednego," yet "Shadrach, Meshach, and Abednego fell down bound into the midst of the burning fiery furnace." Did you catch that? The men who bound the Hebrew boys were only near the flames and died, yet the Hebrew boys were thrown into the flames and lived. By all standards, they should have died outside the furnace along with the king's mighty men. I don't deny the miracle that took place in the furnace, because clearly, God showed up, but unmistakable there was also a miracle on their way to the furnace.

We often rejoice and retell the miracle of the blind man in John 9 who, in obedience to the voice of Jesus and after washing in the pool of Siloam, miraculously received his sight. Yet, might I say that there was another miracle that happened first. It was a miracle in and of itself that this man even made it to the pool! It is believed that he, completely blind and perhaps even in pain from the mud in his eyes, embarked on a seventy yard journey from the temple to the pool. This man who was limited and always dependent upon others made the journey alone. Or was he alone? Perhaps there was a miracle before the miracle we remember. The sustaining Word of God accompanied him as he obediently followed Christ's command.

Remember the story of the four friends who lowered their lame friend through the roof to the feet of Jesus, where he was healed. It's a simple thought, but consider how difficult it must have been to carry a lame man up a ladder without dumping him out or falling from the ladder. They pressed through jeering crowds and overcame obstacles. Surely it was a miracle that their friend made it onto the rooftop, much less to the feet of the Healer!

I look back on our journey and conclude with confidence that there have been many miracles, not only at this church and that church, this revival and that revival, but along the journey from place to place, not just at the destination, but the moments in between. Beginning at Bozeman and ending with chocolate cake on my twenty-seventh birthday, I will never forget; I have a testimony: Jesus never fails.

CHAPTER FOUR

behold.
elijah is here

"It must be nice to live on one big, never-ending vacation," they say. I know they mean well, but life is never a never ending getaway, even for the full-time traveler. There are pros and cons to everything. In the excitement of being an evangelist wife, I have chosen to hardly notice the cons within our lifestyle and instead dwell on the blessings that far outnumber the burdens and battles. That being said, one unfortunate side-effect of full-time travel is having to sometimes miss birthday parties, weddings of loved ones, graduations, and baby showers. I have shed tears in the back of the motorhome because we were parked in a church parking lot nearly a thousand miles away while a family celebration was happening. Other times I deeply miss the community of friends and the building of relationships that can only be created by staying in one place.

Yet, the rich rewards of a traveler's life are priceless to me even still. We live our lives in confidence that, for this season, this is where God has called us to be. He always makes up for those missed moments. That's what is wonderful about serving Him: He is a personal God. We have made friends all over the United States and often do consecutive night revivals, which can last up to a week or more at times. In those cases, I become very attached to the pastor's family. It is always a bittersweet moment when we must pack up the RV at the revival's end and move on to the next church. I seem to always leave a piece of my heart in every place, yet my heart remains full as I reminisce of the conversations and memories we shared.

Evangelizing has taught me that it is not the number of days spent with a person that deems appropriate the definition of friend; it is the trust, loyalty, and camaraderie that is mutually shared between one another. Time and again I have recognized that lonely look in the eye of one who needs only one thing—a friend. No one is excluded from this desire deep within our heart.

Whether they be near or far, a friend is a friend no matter how many miles lie between them. As a part of our nature, and regardless of personality differences, to some extent we all yearn for heart to heart conversations, we anxiously desire to experience joy that can be shared with others, and we are all encouraged with a day of laughter. There is no better way to face the emotional mountains of life than together, with God and a godly friend. From conversation and friendship we draw deep from the well of encouragement and strength. I dare not count the memories I have of riding in the backseat with a pastor's wife, while our husbands talk up front. They swap sermon thoughts, chat about books and whatever kind of meat they smoked last. Our backseat conversations are so very different but often leave me encouraged to know that she has felt what I feel. She has experienced the same emotions, fears, and concerns that I have experienced. As it happens, I'm not crazy at all! She has walked the path I called my own and has too felt the feelings I thought were mine alone. Having friends and seeing what friendships can do, whether we be in Idaho, Georgia, or anywhere in between, I have decided to be a better friend and create in me a source of joy, strength, and encouragement for others.

BIBLICAL FRIENDSHIP

What a beautiful picture of friendship is drawn by the narrative in the fifth chapter of Luke's Gospel. We read the story of a man who is lame, but he had friends. He had true friends. These four friends carried their lame friend until they arrived at the feet of Jesus. This was not some casual good deed done because they were bored and looking for a way to busy their drab day. This was a task that required physical, spiritual, mental, and emotional determination. With a passionate persistence that burned hotter than the sun above, they gladly gave their own strength and carried one, who could not carry himself, to the feet of the Healer. Can you imagine it? They never stopped gripping the corners of the bed which held their friend as they bustled through busy streets, pushed past throngs of people, climbed the shaky ladder that led to the rooftop, tore a large hole in the roof above where Jesus preached, which brought them to the place they were positioned for the miracle. Without cowering down to the rude and harsh words of both saint and sinner, they lowered him down through the gaping hole through which they could see the healing Man from Galilee. Which part is most miraculous? Often we focus only on the miracle of his sins being forgiven and his lame body being healed, yet there is also a level of the miraculous found within the friendship of those four who positioned this man for a divine encounter. True friendship is miraculous. It is selfless. It is Christ-like. God holds friendship in such high regard that He calls himself a friend of men. When the lame man was unable to help himself or act in such faith as would produce his own healing, his friends made the difference. Strangers would have never given so much of their time and energy. One would be hard pressed to find one stranger willing to carry a man across town, up a ladder, through a hole, and down into a crowded house, much less four of them that would work together toward a common cause never receiving anything for themselves.

These friends poured out compassion that mirrored that of Jesus, Who instead of just feeling sorry for a less fortunate soul, was moved into action to lead the helpless one. When his friends took insurmountable moves past the odds and excuses that were readily available, they sowed seeds of faith. And when seeing the faith of those friends, Jesus forgave his sins, healed his body, and commanded him to take up his bed and walk.

Suddenly this new man had an empty bed, a body full of strength, and a joy unspeakable. He was then equipped to go find someone else who was faithless and unable to stand and bring them to the one who had made him whole. He suddenly had the God-given strength to help someone else in a situation like his. He once needed a friend, now he was able to be a friend. What a testimony of encouragement and hope. When there is a miraculous change in our lives, we are not meant to keep it, nor the One who made the difference , to ourselves. We are not merely changed, healed, and made new to live a better and self-centered life: We are made new to help others! Paul tells us in Romans 15:1 (NIV), "We who are strong ought to bear with the failings of the weak and not to please ourselves."

JOB'S TRUE FRIEND

In contrast to the intentional care of the lame man's friends, we find Job, in the darkest days of his life, surrounded by his three friends. The moment starts out with great encouragement, for sometimes there are no words needed, only presence. And then, Eliphaz, surely the extrovert of the group who cannot handle silence too long, piped up. If nothing more than to fill the air and hear himself talk, he began. He began with flattery, reminding Job he has been a source of strength to others around him. But within the next sentence, he reminds Job that no innocent or upright man has ever perished nor been cut off. Soon, his second friend piped up, not only agreeing, but adding to the gloom and doom of condemnation. "God will not take the hand of evildoers!" And then, the third friend spoke. "Job, if iniquity is in your hand, put it away! Don't let your wickedness reside in your dwelling place!" How quickly the conversation had escalated with beginning as a compliment of strength, now holding accusations that Job had brought on his pain by his own sin. And yet, in Job's weakness, he was much stronger than his friends, for he had the capacity to refuse the self-condemning accusations of his own sin his friends had thrust upon him. Job held to his only true friend in that moment, God. No, Job didn't understand why God was allowing him to experience such physical and emotional turmoil, yet his understanding of friendship with God was not clouded. What voices were his friends listening to, because when one listens to God, there is no condemnation, for there is no condemnation in Christ.

Friends will either bring you to the feet of Jesus or lead you

67

to the point of self condemnation. The truth is, the latter is not a friend. Enemies of the soul are those who lead hearts away from the Master. It brings us to the unavoidable question: What kind of friend are we? Has our presence warmed the heart of the heartbroken, or brought a frosty chill by the words we have spoken?

We are all called to be a friend, first to God and then to others. The reality is we are unable to be a good friend to others until we first have a friendship with our God. Knowing and befriending Him is to be like Him, formed unto His image, and fashioned in His likeness. A friend of God takes on the character and Spirit of God. Godly attributes of a friend are surely not hard to identify: encouragement, wisdom, guidance, empathy, sympathy, patience, kindness, celebration, praise, compassion, loyalty, acts of service. Yes, those are actions of a true friend.

On the contrary, jealousy, lying, bitterness, back biting, and selfishness were the sins of Christ's enemies. When we allow those things to infiltrate our friendships, they will always be contrary to the Word, voice, and Spirit of God. True friendships are free from selfishness and offense. Those characteristics only cause pain, division, and deep emotional scars. Jesus is that friend of all friends who brings help in sorrow, healing in His timing and His way, and joy for the journey. Anything against the character of God is against the true definition of friend.

BEHOLD, ELIJAH IS HERE

One quiet afternoon while sitting on my couch and contently spending time in personal devotion, a Scripture jumped out at me in a new way.

"And he answered him, I am: go, tell thy lord, Behold, Elijah is here."
1 Kings 18:8

I took a second look at the verses following and clearly saw that everything changed once the announcement was made, "Behold, Elijah is here."

How well we know that Jesus showing up anywhere makes all the difference, but this was Elijah, just a man, yet a man anointed of God and led by divine instruction. We can identify with this because there have been times when we felt relief and peace by the simple arrival and presence of a parent, loved one, or friend who showed up in the moment we needed them.

When I was engaged to my husband, an aggravated back and neck injury had driven me to the emergency room. I was doing my best to endure the intense pain from muscle spasms, which could be seen on the surface by looking at my neck. Weary from fighting constant pain and crippling fear, I will never forget the moment I learned that my future husband had jumped on an airplane and would be arriving in a few hours to be with me. When my parents announced he was there, everything changed. Somehow I knew I would be okay. He held me in his strong arms, sympathized with my suffering, and brought comfort simply by his presence.

The presence of some mean everything, but the presence of others bring nothing but despair. As for some, their presence would not help or guide, warm or cheer, comfort or inspire. Some people are little more than another face in the crowd, someone else showing up to the party, only to leave again without making a difference at all. How sad to think of a life that is lived without touching the life of another. It convicts me to think of the people I have brushed by who were hurting, yet in my haste I did not help them. How many people have noticed me and earnestly hoped that I would share a smile, speak a kind word, or put a tremble in the step of their enemy, yet I never noticed them?

When Elijah arrived, the atmosphere changed, and everyone took notice. The scene instantly became more dramatic. Peace was brought to the hearts of those who strove for truth, evildoers momentarily laid down their antics, those working in the enemy's camp were stricken with a fear of defeat, while comfort was bestowed upon the pure in heart. Let it also be said that without the presence of God that accompanied Elijah, there would be no peace to pass along or power to overcome an adversary. It was not Elijah's manhood or humanity that accomplished those things. Such can only happen by the Spirit of God that dwells inside a man. We can only give that which we have available.

So let me shine some light on the scene that is set in the eighteenth chapter of 1 Kings. The prophet Elijah had pronounced judgment upon Israel by way of a God ordained drought. For three and a half years it did not rain. The entire land was suffering as a result of the idolaters who brought upon all of them the judgment of God. When desperation reached its highest peak, and they could no longer tolerate the parched predicament in which they were in, the wicked King Ahab set out in a ravenous search for water. The king's servant Obadiah, also set out to find water but found Elijah instead. When the prophet saw Obadiah, he instructed the servant to go tell the king, "Behold, Elijah is here."

For the first time in three and a half years, there was hope for a brighter day. Those four words seemed to bring a flood of hope. A glimmer of light which signaled the end was suddenly seen because there was now someone who could touch God.

What a friend he was to the righteous, just by his courage and the presence of God that accompanied him. I sat back after only a few minutes of study, convicted and stirred, wondering what implications and meaning would be communicated if my name was put in the place of Elijah's. Should someone say, "Jamin is here," I pray that God will help me to make a difference while I am there. What would my presence mean?

THE PRESENCE OF GOD

To say "Elijah is here" was to say that God had shown up in the midst of trial, grief, and sorrow, not that he was God, but that God was with him.

An epoch moment in Elijah's life proved this to be true. It was after Elijah had come down from the mountain where God had miraculously provided water at the brook Cherith and food from a raven's mouth to sustain the prophet. Drought had consumed the land as a result of Elijah's prophetic utterance, yet God took care of his own and divinely provided his every need. Elijah was surely comforted by the undeniable presence and provision of God as he sat next to the brook and partook of the bread and water. Every sip of cool clear water must have reminded him that God would not leave nor forsake him. Every meal delivered from the mouth of the raven testified of God's faithfulness. In time, even the brook dried up. Elijah was then directed by God to go into the town of Zaraphath where he would encounter a woman who would sustain him.

Behold, Elijah Is Here

Elijah found her gathering firewood. The prophet said, "Fetch me, I pray thee, a little water in a vessel, that I may drink" (1 Kings 17:10). This selfless woman quickly hurried off to fulfill his wishes and yet before she disappeared completely, he called out one more request. "Will you also bring me a morsel of bread in your hand?" A small drink of water was one thing, but the bread was too much. Throwing up her hands, she felt the bitter sting of her despairing reality. She, who had anxiously hastened to care for the man of God's first request, now hopelessly hesitates at even the thought of fulfilling his second request. With passion and pain she cried, "As the Lord your God lives, I have not a cake, but only a handful of meal in a barrel, and a little oil in a cruse. Behold, I am gathering two sticks that I may go in and make it for me and my son, that we may eat, and die."

But Elijah spoke. He echoed to her the same words that had been previously spoken to him by God; "Fear not." So often does God repeat those words to humanity. We seem to never learn and yet he seems to never cease calling us out of fear's torment. Three hundred and sixty-five times is that directive spoken in the Bible, ensuring we have a "fear not" for every day of the year! Elijah's arrival was symbolic in the sense that he brought with him the comforting, although sometimes uncomfortable, Word of God. He had been known to be God's mouthpiece; therefore Elijah's presence was a symbol that God was also present.

Surely that Zaraphath widow saw beyond the fatal potential of her following the prophet's direction and could sense the presence and power of God that enveloped his unexpected command. She obeyed, and in this dry barren land, God honored her obedience by miraculously multiplying the meal and oil that should have been depleted. As God did for her, he does for us today. He brings provision, kindness, and comfort into our lives through others. His Word comes to us through the mouth of a man of God. His kindness is reflected in the love of a brother or sister. His provision is performed in the sensitivity of others to His Spirit in the hour of our greatest need. What God did for Elijah at the brook Cherith was done through Elijah for the Zaraphath widow and her son. It's true, what we receive from God is intended for us to share with others. Behold, Elijah is here! What comfort, kindness and provision accompanied the man who was led by the Spirit of God.

Kind words and actions live on forever. I imagine Elijah spoke many kind and comforting words to that precious woman and her son in those weeks and months that followed. Around the supper table, while cleaning, doing chores, or sitting around an evening fire, there must have been a sense of security and peace just knowing that Elijah was there. More importantly, God was there! There is much comfort found in the presence of a heart that is filled with God's Spirit. His Spirit is our comforter and His people ought always bring His comforting Spirit with them everywhere they go!

THE WORD OF GOD

To say "Elijah is here" is to say that there is still law and divine retribution at work in the world. It means that there is still a godly standard of righteousness. It means there is someone standing up for the truths and principles of the Word of God. Throughout the life story of Elijah we see the biblical truth that God's eyes are upon the wicked and, although we question God's inactivity toward evil at times, the wicked will never go unpunished. Even when it appeared that righteousness had been removed and ungodliness ruled under the reign of Ahab and Jezebel, God was still on His throne. Baal, their false god, had been propped up throughout the nation and become a normal sight to behold. Those wicked rulers had purposed to make evil so common in their culture that people would become desensitized to the utter horror of their hellish agenda. Any opportunity, big or small, to prop up an idol of Baal in the eyes of the children and make it appear glamorous and attractive was all done with much intention and calculation. Worshipers of Jehovah were mocked, persecuted, and threatened with both force and fear in an effort to remove God from their nation. Yet the evil men and women seem to forget God cannot be removed, nor can the wicked escape the infallible truths and judgments of His Word. Therefore, Elijah's presence meant more than could be seen on the surface. Not only had he arrived, but he had brought with him the Word and judgments of God. The prophet's presence seemed to say, "Baal had better bow. Every false god had better tremble at the power of Him who is above all."

We each need the courage of Elijah. To stand for something, to stand for anything automatically means that we are also against something. The one who stands for godliness angers the ungodly. Righteousness infuriates unrighteousness. Holiness frustrates the unholy. Although we are commanded to love, to love evil is always the exception.

To say Elijah is here meant that God had not forsaken His people and that judgment had come upon that wicked nation and its wicked king. Elijah appeared unto King Ahab and pronounced when he would die and that it would be in the place where the dogs licked up the blood of Naboth and so would they lick up his blood also.

Time passed and appeared as though the wicked King had somehow escaped judgment or Elijah had misfired his words. However, one unassuming day Ahab went up to battle with Jehoshaphat, King of Judah. In the midst of chariots rolling to and fro and armies moving into position, surely then at the location of the proclaimed judgment, Ahab must have remembered Elijah's haunting words concerning his end. Taking off his royal robes, Ahab chose to disguised himself as a soldier. Yet God recognizes his creation whether we are disguised or not; God is not fooled by our meager attempts to cover up evil character and hidden identities. God is truth and sees truth for what it is. During the course of that battle, a man used by God brought up his bow and let go an arrow that smote King Ahab, in spite of his armor of protection. When the sun had set, the king died from his wound, and just as had been prophesied, the dogs, in the place where Naboth had laid, licked the blood of King Ahab on the floor of his chariot.

Behold, Elijah is here. Even in the wicked day and evil generation in which we now live all these centuries later, there are still people of God, like Elijah, who willingly and courageously stand in the gap for the sake of righteousness. Not everyone has succumbed to the sin of our day. Not everyone has compromised. Not everyone has been deceived by the godless agenda or culture. Not everyone has been desensitized by the blatant and praised presence of idols. There are still those who boldly stand for truth, preaching righteousness and proclaiming God's Word. In God's timing, judgment will unmistakably come to the evil, and yet the righteous shall live forever.

THE POWER OF PRAYER

To say "Elijah is here" is to say prayer is being made.

"Confess your faults one to another, and pray one for another, that ye may be healed. The effectual fervent prayer of a righteous man availeth much. Elias was a man subject to like passions as we are, and he prayed earnestly that it might not rain: and it rained not on the earth by the space of three years and six months. And he prayed again, and the heaven gave rain, and the earth brought forth her fruit."
James 5:16-18

It was Elijah's prayer that had ceased the rain, and now Elijah could pray again with confidence for the release of abundant rain. On the mount, he drenched the wood with water, then prayed this prayer: "Hear me, o Lord, that the people may know you are Lord God..." Elijah had confidence not only in his prayers, but in the God who answers prayer. He knew in whom he had placed his faith, and his heart was indeed for Jehovah to be glorified.

I dare not liken myself to the stature of Elijah, but I too have confidence in my prayers. He has answered too many personal prayers for me to doubt his ability to move in miraculous ways. "Jesus, give me the grace to forgive her." He did. "Jesus, I need this job desperately. Let me know the job is mine before the interview is over." He did. "Jesus, I'm exhausted and do not want to go. Give me strength and joy for the journey." He did. "Jesus, I'm asking you to take this pain away right now, in your name! You are my healer!" He did. "Jesus, my school bill must be paid off by the end of Christmas break, and I need the money to go back to Bible school! My heart desires to learn more of you, Jesus." He did it. "Jesus, I desire a husband who loves you and loves me. I desire a good man who is fun, loves ministry, and is full of life…" Oh, He did it! Granted, there are some prayers that seem to go unanswered, yet I will take his "no" or "not yet" and trust that He knows what I do not and can see what I cannot see. His track record has proved Him to be trustworthy. I trust Him because He has never failed me.

Elijah's presence meant that prayer unto God was being made. How about our presence? What does our showing up communicate to those around us? Does our presence mean there will be prayer? Would your friends scoff at the very idea of you attending pre-service prayer before church? Would it be rare to find you on your knees praying in your bedroom? Would there be laughter at the thought of you gathering your peers to petition God in times of trial? It reminds me of something that took place in college, which shall be forever branded into my memory. There was a handsome, likable fellow in my friend group one semester that I would sometimes hang out with. One particular Wednesday evening, upon arriving at church early for pre-service prayer, someone saw me and asked if my friend was there too. Someone else chimed up, "Maybe he's in the prayer room?" At that question, an entire row of Bible college students erupted in laughter as one of them honestly said, "There is no way he is here early for pre-service prayer." It shook me because it was true. I pulled away quickly after that night because the saying echoed in my ears: "Show me who your friends are, and I will show you who you will be in five years." You become who your friends are. He was not a bad guy, but I knew that prayer was too important to risk being influenced by someone who was known by a lack of prayer.

I have learned to love and long for prayer. It has proven to be my joy on sunny days and my peace in the passing but very much present storm. Prayer is unique in the way that you don't openly share how often or how much you pray. A prayer life isn't something to be worn as a badge. Prayer is easily identified in ones actions, spirit, fruit, and character. People can tell if a person has been with Jesus or not. When tragedy strikes and you begin to pray, people can tell if you are uncomfortably praying out of panic or confidently praying out of faith. They know you have a deeply-personal relationship with Jesus because a friend of God always reflects the pure and holy character of their Friend.

God never tires of hearing your voice. It comes to Him as a sweet savor. The truth be told, the people around us are encouraged to know they have someone who is able to touch heaven on their behalf. As for me, when I am uncomfortable, afraid, or hurting, I long for a godly friend who will come along beside me and touch heaven with me. I look for an Elijah in my life whose presence brings with it a confidence that prayer will be offered and God will surely hear their voice. In fact, I pray I can find Elijah within myself.

THE CERTAINTY OF LIFE ETERNAL

To say "Elijah is here" is to realize that there is certainty of a future and glory of a life to come. To put it simply, godly men live forever!

In a moment of inquiry Jesus asked his disciples, "Whom do men say that I, the son of man, am?" Oh, some say you are the prophet Jeremiah, and some say you are Elijah come back to earth. Elijah! Of course we know that Jesus was not the old prophet, yet the comparison and association in their minds prove that a godly life should show forth fruits of righteousness and ultimately resemble Christ. Elijah had long been whisked away in the chariot of fire, but his reputation lived on. When God manifested himself in flesh and was finally visibly seen by men, their failed attempts to discover His true identity led some to consider, "Is Elijah here again?" Peter made clear the truth concerning Jesus' identity when he declared, "Thou art the Christ, the Son of the living God." Nevertheless, when seeing Jesus, they thought of Elijah.

When Peter, James, John, and Jesus ascended the mountain, there, while the disciples slept, Jesus prayed and was transfigured before them, his countenance so translucent and filled with the glory of heaven. When the disciples finally awoke, they were utterly amazed to see not only Jesus before them but Moses and Elijah also standing next to and talking with the Savior. Proving those who live in Christ, truly live forever! God is the God of the living and not the dead! He cares so much about us that He has made a way for us to escape our greatest fear: death. When we live for Christ and are filled with His Spirit, just as they were on the day of Pentecost, we have the promise of eternal life with Christ. Though seeing the old prophet only temporarily on the Mount of

Behold, Elijah Is Here

Transfiguration, I wonder if Peter might have impulsively spoken those powerful words, "Behold, Elijah is here!"

BEHOLD, YOU ARE HERE

The hurting heart does not care how fashionable we are or how attractive we look; it desires strength from someone stronger than itself. A hurting person only wants a shoulder to cry on, a friend to lean on, a hand to hold. They crave comfort and kindness, which is found ultimately in God's Word and through His Spirit. Hope is what the hurting heart is in need of, and Jesus is that hope.

In the time of trial, all else fades away except strong character. There is no desire for a presence who brings outward beauty alone. There is no call to the selfish one because a selfish heart is never truly available to others. Godly character in us is what the hurting are hoping to find. How true it is that character is more visible than talent and anointing. The more I see of people, the more I admire their character and not their talent. Who cares how good one can play an instrument or sing a song if they lack the ability to look beyond their own pride and help a broken heart? God is not impressed with credentials, titles, positions, or status. He is only impressed with character. And at the end of the day, so are people.

I have found this to be true—the end of a life, no one ever really talks about the external. They say, "They were always there for me. They prayed with me when I was hurting. They answered my call when I needed them. They showed up when no one else did. They loved me when I made a mistake."

Our prayers never die. Our forgiveness is never forgotten. Our kind and encouraging words echo as an anchor in other's storms. I desperately want it to be said of me that my presence means prayer. I want not only the enemy of my soul, but also friends, to know that I will touch heaven on their behalf. I want the world to know where I stand. I love righteousness, and I will stand against evil. I want my presence to be accompanied by the comfort of the Holy Ghost. But alas, it is only possible if I am completely devoted to God and filled with His Spirit.

If traveling has shown me anything, it is the assurance that there are modern day Elijah's in this generation. They are present. They are kind. They are selfless. They are warriors of prayer. They are filled with God's Spirit and stand in the gap for the lost. Do not be discouraged. You, my dear reader, have more of Elijah in you than you realize. You have the heart to pray for your family, friends, and even enemies. You have the courage to stand for holiness and righteousness though it be unpopular in our ever worsening sinful world. You have the compassion to extend the kindness of God to those around you. You have the blessed hope and the promise of heaven. I have prayed that every reader who holds this book in their hand would be reminded, in spite of the spiritually dry and barren state of our culture, "Behold, you are here!" What a difference you make.

CHAPTER FIVE

lessons from a coddiwomple

"A coddiwomple?!"

I nearly hollered out my new found word. We were driving to our next revival in Idaho. I had taken a break from my fixation on the beautiful scenery through which we drove, and I looked down at the scrapbooking stickers in my lap that I planned to use in documenting our trip memories. One of the stickers read, "Coddiwomple life is for me." I had never heard that strange word but was intrigued enough to look it up. To be a coddiwomple simply means, "To travel purposely towards a vague or unknown destination." Looking further into this newly discovered word, I found that it is more than a word. It is a movement. People are giving up their jobs, selling their homes, leaving behind friends, family and neighbors to set out on a minimalistic and nomadic lifestyle with only a tent and as much as can fit into a backpack. You could call them a traveler, but coddiwomple describes them best. They travel without plans of a destination. Each day is new and all for itself. There is no specific location at which they strive to arrive. Their only real plan is to not have one. They could end up anywhere, or they could end up going nowhere at all.

There is a part of that lifestyle that sounds appealing and all too relatable to the life of a full-time evangelist. Some of our most memorable moments have been those spontaneous turns off the highway and unplanned adventures, but we always had an ultimate destination. It bogs down my mind to think that people willingly live from day to day with no conceivable idea of where they will lay their head. Isn't it the promised beauty of a future destination that persuades our feet to go further? I have been on many hikes where the alluring draw of misty waterfalls and rock arches with mountainous backdrops were what convinced my weary feet to take the next step onward. How easy it must be to turn back when you've caught no glimpse of the future or felt no excitement of the destination that awaits you!

It is the same in our walk with God on the journey to our eternal reward. As children of God, why do we so easily allow our minds to rush past the splendor of our heavenly home that awaits? Although we have never been there, the child of God has faith to believe His words.

> *"And if I go and prepare a place for you, I will come again, and receive you unto myself; that where I am, there ye may be also."*
> *John 14:3*

To have faith in all the other promises that pertain to the here and now, but none in those of the by and by, is to walk aimlessly through life without any joy or delight of what lies beyond the grave. The enemy has made it his purpose to market heaven as an undesirable and unrealistic place, to the end that we would forsake all motivation to continue passionately onward. If heaven isn't real and this world is all there is, how easy and reasonable it would be to choose the temporary pleasures sin offers. When heaven becomes undesirable, sin becomes all the more appealing. But since when has the holy, pure presence of God become undesirable? As if the lake, which is described as being clear as glass, or streets of pure gold are not motivation enough, when did earthly experiences become more appealing than an eternal experience in the presence of the Lamb that sits upon the throne? If we do not enjoy His presence here on earth, how can we expect to receive the honor of experiencing it eternally in that place He has prepared?

Satan understands the splendor of heaven all too well and, since he will never be welcomed back into the heavenly glory, He will stop at nothing to secure the loss of our same glorious experience. He knows that trust in God's promise and a glimpse through faith of what awaits us just over in the glory land is more than enough to sustain us along the journey. No bump in the road will detour us from our destination. How easy it would be to take the wide road if we are not convinced the narrow road of Truth is worth it. Jesus taught us in Matthew 7:14, "Straight is the gate, and narrow is the way, which leads unto life, and few there be that find it."

No, there is not a lot of sparkle, glitz, or glamour along the narrow road, but we must not be enticed by the sensual allure nets of this world. Our eyes must not be drawn to the temporal, fading flashes of false hope. We must fix our eyes upon Him Who leads us, Whose hand we hold, and Whose Word we head. On this narrow road is the promise of His light brightening our path. Psalm 16:11 says, "Thou wilt shew me the path of life: in thy presence is fulness of joy, at thy right hand there are pleasures for evermore."

Lessons From A Coddiwomple

To see Yellowstone, the Smoky Mountains, the Grand Tetons, and the Rockies is to stand in awe of God's creation, yet it could not begin to scratch the surface of the celestial beauty that He has prepared for His church. The beautiful sights and scenery of our great country are undisputedly trumped by just one moment in a service where God's glory fills the house. How I weep with wonder and joy in His presence! Those are moments that no words or social media post could capture. My collection of national park postcards prove how beautiful God has made this world in which we live, but His glory proves why we live. We find life more abundant in His presence and, once you have experienced that, nothing but His Spirit will satisfy your soul. To me, this narrow road is a beautiful road. On this road I am never alone. On this road I am led by an unseen hand. On this road I am traveling to a place beyond compare.

We often sing and speak of what we love, our words keeping it alive in our minds. So I will sing of where I'm going! I will thank God for the blessed hope He has given and keep it at the forefront of my remembrance. I am less likely to fall into sin and believe the lies of the adversary if I am speaking of salvation and declaring the Word of God. I believe with all of my heart, just as all of His other promises have proven true, so shall it be with the promise of heaven. That is the destination that must be kept before us.

Yet, I can learn a thing or two from a coddiwomple. For this journey itself ought to be one of joy, excitement, and adventure. We must never lose sight of our goal, but oh, what memories can be made in the meantime. Through the stories of our journey, God reminds me that life is an adventure and there is joy. Here is what I've learned from the life of a coddiwomple: Anything can happen.

THE HANDLEBAR MUSTACHE

Jeremy and I are often asked, "Has anything funny ever happened while you are preaching?" One of my favorite stories to tell happened on a Sunday night at a church in Ohio. We had never been there before, so meeting the pastor and his wife before the service was enjoyable. They were so kind and welcoming to us. We all had great expectation of what God would do that evening. Service began and I quickly noticed that it was a lively church. I thought all the more, "This could really be good tonight!"

After the pastor introduced and welcomed us to the pulpit, we sang a few songs, and Jeremy began to preach what he felt God had given him for that service. He had been preaching about fifteen or twenty minutes when I realized that something strange had happened. About the time I noticed, the congregation also noticed. It wasn't that his shirt collar was sticking up, his pant leg was caught in his sock, or his hair out of place. Those things are nearly expected to happen in a Pentecostal church. This was much worse and far more confusing. I looked intently and what I saw was unbelievable. My husband had grown a handlebar mustache while he was preaching! How could this be? I had seen him shave that morning, and I knew that nobody could grow a full mustache in fifteen minutes. I looked closely and realized that the black wind screen that was on the microphone was old and peeling. Tiny pieces of black fuzz were wearing off onto my Jeremy's lip. He had no idea what had happened, except that the congregation wasn't real engaged in his message. He later told me, "They seemed to be distracted by something." That something was a black fuzzy handlebar shaped mustache.

89

Lessons From A Coddiwomple

In an attempt to overcome the unknown distraction, Jeremy left the pulpit and platform and began walking the altar area. The more he felt disconnected from the audience, the closer to them he would get. Soon, I saw the young people on the front row begin to snicker and laugh. They had seen what I had seen. Jeremy could sense something was happening but was determined to preach through it. The longer he preached and the closer he got to the congregation, the more people began to notice his "facial hair."

There has never been a time when I was more embarrassed, frustrated, and ready to explode with emotion. I wanted so badly to get up from my seat, interrupt the service, and tell him what was going on! I felt so sorry for my husband, who was completely oblivious to the artificial hair-growth. I was frustrated because the distraction was putting a damper on the service and hindering people from receiving what was being preached. I didn't know what to do. About that time the pastor's wife leaned over to me and asked, "Did your husband have a mustache before church?" "No," I replied, "the wind screen is wearing off and sticking to his face." From that moment until the end of service, I tried to subtly get Jeremy's attention without interrupting the sermon, but it didn't work. The mustache was there to stay.

After church we stood around the edge of the platform laughing. The pastor admitted, "I kept looking and thinking, I didn't notice him having a mustache before church!" Unfortunately, it was far from the best service we have ever had, but it is one of the most memorable. Those people will never remember that service by how many received the Holy Ghost, how many were baptized in Jesus Name, or how many were healed. They will remember that Sunday night for no other reason but that the evangelist grew a perfectly groomed handlebar mustache in fifteen minutes.

What could I say? Poor Jeremy, what could he say? There was nothing to be said but much to laugh about. None of us should take ourselves so seriously. Sometimes we just have to laugh at yourselves. Laughter is a part of the journey!

THE COFFEE STAIN

It pains me to write it, but it's true. I can be clumsy. Oh, I try not to! In fact, sometimes when I try the hardest I end up being the clumsiest. Spilled coffee? I have done it. You have done it. We have all done it! Yet there is a vast difference between spilling it on the counter or on the floor and spilling it on a lovely pastor's wife. I'm ashamed to admit it, but I did. The pastor and his wife, who we love, had taken Jeremy and me to an amazing local coffee and sandwich shop. We ordered fall flavored lattes and grilled sandwiches and then sat down at a table to visit. I was ecstatic. Discovering new coffee shops is one of my favorite things to do, especially when we are taken there by people we love. As we waited for our names to be called, we sipped on our coffees and shared in conversation. Before I go any further in this story, you need to get a mental picture of the outfit that the pastor's wife was wearing. She, herself, is pure class. That day she was wearing a stunning champaign pink business blazer. It looked to be warm in the chilly fall weather but beyond that, it was one of the most stunning jackets I've ever seen. It looked like something Princess Kate might wear. I had admired it all day, but when I raised my hands to dramatically tell a story, it happened. My hand hit my coffee cup, which caused coffee to shoot up out of the moving cup, only to land directly on that stunning champaign pink jacket. Two of my favorite things had just been united: that jacket and a pumpkin spice latte. I loved them both, but they don't belong together. I was wearing a boring, black turtleneck. Why couldn't the coffee have spilled on me? I would've been embarrassed still, but instead I was mortified as that precious pastor's wife began scrubbing her blazer with a wet wipe. Apologizing seemed to be so shallow, yet she was gracious and convinced me that she could get the stain out. I wanted to crawl under the table but knew I'd probably spill something else if I did that.

That night, after the revival service, they invited us to their home for fellowship and a meal. I had been in the house no time at all when I quickly spotted the jacket draped over the back of a dining room chair to dry. To my delight and relief, she informed me that the stain had come out! Alas, the beautiful champaign pink blazer had been restored to its original beauty. I was so thankful. Yet, more than that the stain had come out, I was thankful for her grace and kindness when this young, clumsy, evangelist's wife nearly ruined her beautiful outfit. I've heard it said that actions, might I say "reactions," speak louder than words. Two people taught me two things that day. First, I taught myself to never do that again. Secondly, that precious woman of God taught me how to be gracious and forgiving.

MY FAVORITE PIZZA PARTY

There have been a few memorable occasions when, while parked in a new area, we order pizza from a local shop and have a pizza party in the RV. By "party" I mean that I squeak in excited glee and do a little dance around the motorhome while Jeremy remains calm and retains enough dignity for both of us. He's good at that. We rarely eat pizza, but when we do, we order the same two kinds: an all meat pizza for Jeremy and a thin crust buffalo chicken pizza for me. I suppose the rarity of our pizza parties is what makes them memorable to me.

In the beginning of 2021, our preaching schedule brought us back to Tupelo, Mississippi. It was a very quiet day. I picked up my morning coffee from a local shop, Jeremy and I had a beautiful prayer time together, then I started the dreadful task of cleaning house. Thankfully, it doesn't take long in a thirty-seven foot RV. I then went on a walk outside. Looking back on that moment, I vividly remember my emotions that day as I walked. Even with the blue sky above and the warm sun shining down, my mood was clouded. I felt as if I was not doing enough. I felt an inner tug of war. I felt self-conscious about sharing our life and the joys of traveling on social media because some have misinterpreted our life as being only an extended vacation, yet they don't see the battles we fight and the faith that is required to live on the road. There are spiritual attacks. There are lonely nights spent in "Timbuktu," far from family and friends. We make it great and have loved every second, but there is more to it than what social media tells.

There were things on my daily to-do list, but "I'm not doing enough" was all I heard ringing in my ear that day. In fact, it shouted at me for a couple of days. This was not the first, nor the last time, I had felt these emotions. There aren't many routines to be had for an evangelist. Our daily schedules change from city to city and from church to church. Some weeks we are so busy we hardly sleep, and yet other weeks we just wait for Sunday to roll around. Those weeks are when I sometimes feel purposeless and lazy. This was one of those weeks. I know that feeling isn't original to me, for we all long for purpose and to feel like we're making a difference in the world around us, but I seemed to own those feelings that day. My mind moved as quickly as my feet as I walked and waged this war within myself.

"If I was in Africa as a missionary's wife maybe then I would feel like I'm doing enough." Now I understand the foolishness of that thought, but in the moment I was blinded to reality. It is all too easy for us to fool ourselves into thinking that we'll be content and fulfilled in another place, another setting, and given another set of circumstances. "In a different position, a different calling, and a different ministry roll I could do so much for the Lord" we tell ourselves, yet we fail to consider that someone else is longingly looking at our life the same way we are looking at someone else's. They want our life and we want their life. Then, undoubtedly, we would finally find purpose and fulfillment. Yet, in all of our wanting, do we consider what God wants? Could it be that He has called and equipped us to be where we are, and the enemy is distracting us away from our purpose by luring our attention elsewhere. Instead of being content in the will of God, we give ear to the enemy who tells us that God has forsaken us in our faithfulness.

Exhausted from both walking and weighing out my worth, I retreated to the RV. After a few minutes I heard a knock at the door. There at the foot of our steps stood a man from the local church we had preached at. He held three large boxes of pizza in hand and explained that they were extras that hadn't been touched and would not be eaten. Thinking of us, he grabbed three of them at random and delivered them to our door. We thanked him for his thoughtfulness and as soon as he left, curiously peeked into each box. Jeremy and I were shocked! Two of the three pizza were our favorites, the very ones we always order! All meat for Jeremy and thin crust buffalo chicken pizza for me. Silly? No, I believe God was reminding me that He has His eye upon us, even on the days we feel weary and worthless.

With free food and a pizza party, God seemed to restore my confidence and assurance of where He had put us and what He had called us to do. We were in God's will after all! Contrary to my wandering mind, I wasn't called to the jungles of Africa. My purpose wasn't waiting for me in the far reaches of the globe. My purpose was right in front of me, patiently waiting to be recognized. My calling was clarified. Gone were my thoughts to be elsewhere or to find more purpose in another calling. My doubts vanished, my questions ceased. I was content being assured that God knows where I am, even when I lose myself.

The good news was that there was no cooking or dishes to be done that night. The cleaning had already been done earlier in the day, so I relaxed that evening in the beautiful seventy-degree, Mississippi spring weather overwhelmed that God once again was mindful of me. Solomon described God so big that "the heaven and heaven of heavens cannot contain thee" and yet He takes time to know our pizza order. The clouds are the dust of his feet, but I am the apple of His eye. The pizza wasn't anything special, but knowing how special we were to God made that pizza party one of the most memorable of my life.

Lessons From A Coddiwomple

In a matter of days we packed up and pulled out of Tupelo, headed toward the next revival, with a new perspective of the journey. Every stop bringing us closer to the destination and all the while, knowing God is with us.

THE BILTMORE ESTATE

Tucked away amid the Blue Ridge Mountains, who doesn't want to experience the enchanting beauty of the Biltmore Estate in Asheville, North Carolina? I had dreamed of visiting but hadn't been able to. You can imagine my excitement when, while preaching a five night revival near the coast of Georgia, I realized that we would have to pass through Asheville, North Carolina, that next week in order to get to Pigeon Forge, Tennessee, where we were scheduled to sing at an event called Praise In The Smokies. Jeremy, in his innocence, didn't have a clue about Biltmore, but knowing my desire to go, he surprised me by saying, "To break up the trip, we'll stay overnight at an RV park in Asheville and go visit the Biltmore Estate." I was elated and immediately my mind began to imagine the magical moment this would surely be. Then, suddenly I heard my husband ask, "Is there a cost or is this thing free?" "Oh, no," I thought, "It's anything but free!" I suddenly got sheepish and quiet, because he had brought up the one thing that can make or break any good plan: money.

Sitting in the wooden chairs at Cracker Barrel, I finally worked up the courage to tell him the ticket price. "It costs that much to tour a house?" Jeremy was taken aback. I then educated him on what the Biltmore Estate is. It took much convincing, but he finally agreed to take me since he had already committed as much before realizing the cost. I was overjoyed about going, yet the emotional feeler in me felt bad that it would cost so much for something that my husband could care less about. Suddenly, it hit me. "I'll pray," I said to my husband. He seemed utterly confused, so I continued. "I'll pray someone gives us the money to pay for the tickets!" "Okay, you do that," he responded with a chuckle, not thinking for a second that my prayer just might be answered.

We had a wonderful revival that week. The church was friendly, kind, worshipful, and responsive to the preaching and the presence of God. Visitors seemed to show up every service, and people were receiving the Holy Ghost and being baptized in Jesus Name. Seeing God work in people's lives was well worth the miles we drove to be there and the energy we poured into those services.

The revival ended on Sunday, and when the service was dismissed I made my way to our product table in the foyer. Once most of the people had left, I began to pack up our books and CDs. An elderly woman walked up to me and put some cash into my hand, making sure I knew that it wasn't for a book or a CD. "That's for you and your husband," she said. Only a moment later, a beaming mother and daughter who I had met several nights earlier came up to me with a card. I was moved and could hardly wait to read it! After I packed up, I opened the card. There was cash laying inside the card, accompanied by a precious note that meant so much to me. I couldn't believe it! I totaled up all of the cash I had been given, and it was the exact amount we needed in order to visit the Biltmore Estate the next day.

"Jeremy!" I nearly ran through the church parking lot to get into the motorhome. I hollered in my excited voice the moment we were behind closed doors, "God gave us the money for our Biltmore tickets! I knew He would!" He could only shake his head and smile.

We left early the next morning and saw the Biltmore that afternoon. It was all the more beautiful and special just knowing that God cared enough to provide not only for my needs but my desires. It may seem trivial to some, and I supposed they are entitled to their opinion, but they'll never convince me that God doesn't care about the little things. They'll never convince me that God doesn't put a high value on memorable moments spent together with your spouse, children, or loved ones. They'll never convince me that God isn't able to answer the prayer that others think will never be answered. No, God doesn't always answer my prayers, but He certainly did that day.

When touring the Biltmore Legacy Museum, I was enraptured by a story. Mr. and Mrs. George Vanderbilt, who owned the estate, had planned to sail on the Titanic in 1912. After all, they could afford it, and it was the desired way to travel. To my amazement, the night before their departure, they changed their minds. Mrs. Vanderbilt wrote to her friend, "For no reason whatsoever we decided to sail on the Olympic and had only eighteen hours to get ready. We were homesick, and simply felt we must get home, so we changed our ship, as I say, at the eleventh hour!"

It reminded me that in this eleventh hour in which you and I are living in, just before the coming of the Lord, we must make sure we are on the ship that will get us safely home. The decision to obey the Word of God, repent of our sins, be baptized in Jesus Name, receive the gift of the Holy Ghost, and live a life of holiness unto God in this eleventh hour is able to save you from eternal death and bring you safely into the eternal home we call heaven!

DO YOU HAVE THE ENVELOPE?

We should have known something strange was going to happen while parked at this church when one evening we heard footsteps on our roof. No, it wasn't Santa and his reindeer. It was a little barefoot neighborhood boy. He had scaled our ladder and was touring the top of our RV. We clearly heard the sound of footsteps and then felt the shaking of another boy endeavoring to scale the ladder. Jeremy hurried outside and was extremely gracious, yet still sternly hollered, "Hey, you guys get down from there!" He didn't want to scare them so badly that they fell off the roof or tumbled down the ladder, yet wanted them to understand that this wasn't the new neighborhood playground. This was our home. We laughed as they scurried across the church parking lot and down the street.

In the heart of northern Indiana's Amish country, we were parked at a church in Elkhart. The week was memorable for many reasons, not just because of the rooftop guests. The pastor and wife had treated us with such hospitality and kindness, showing us all of their favorite places in their city. On our first morning there, we woke up to a fresh box of donuts from a local Amish bakery, hand delivered by the pastor himself. With a hot cup of black coffee, they melted in our mouth. Throughout the week we frequented a local coffee shop that is connected to a boutique and repurposed antique store. One afternoon they took us to tour an elaborate early twentieth century home that is still, more than a hundred years later, a wonder of architectural design.

Lessons From A Coddiwomple

On one of our last mornings parked there, my husband and I decided to buy a new leather recliner for the motorhome in a neighboring town. Elkhart County is where most RV's are manufactured; therefore, it is a prime place to find discounted parts and furniture. On the way to the furniture warehouse, I had found a coffee shop that I asked to stop at. Jeremy and I jumped into the car, pulled out of the church parking lot, and drove about twenty five minutes to downtown Goshen, Indiana. It's a small quaint town, surrounded my Amish farming communities. Just blocks away from the coffee shop, while stopped at a stop sign, Jeremy noticed an old Mercury Grand Marquis behind us. Clearly, they, like us, were traveling from Elkhart to Goshen. We assumed that having now arrived in town, we would go our way and they would go theirs. Jeremy turned his left turn signal on and turned in the direction of the coffee shop. That car turned left also, trying not to be alarmed and thinking, "Surely we are not being followed."

We arrived at our destination, and Embassy Coffee Company sat on the north side of the street. Traveling from the west, we were on the south side of the street and rather than park and walk across traffic, Jeremy decided to test this scenario one more time to see if we were truly being followed. He drove just past the coffee shop and then did a u-turn, parking next to the curb just a couple of spaces down from the Embassy Coffee Company door. He put the car in park, and we anxiously looked into our mirrors to see if the Mercury had made its way on through the next intersection. What we feared might be possible, was definitely true. The driver of that car made an identical u-turn behind us and parked next to the same curb about thirty feet behind our silver Honda. We were being followed!

I could hardly process what was happening but knew I didn't like it. Jeremy stayed just as calm as he always does. We hurried out of our car and into the coffee shop. Just before stepping through the doorway, we looked back over our shoulder to see if our follower was coming to buy our coffee. Emerging from that faded four door car was a tall women, probably in her early or mid sixties. She wore a long skirt that fit loosely and flared out from her feet when we walked: her hair wildly escaping her pulled back bun. "Well, she looks innocent enough," I thought. For a moment I thought that maybe this was all in our heads and there would be a reasonable explanation. About the time we finished our order and moved down the counter to wait for our drinks, she opened the door and came inside. We looked at her and she looked at us, but we tried our best to make sure our eyes never met with hers. "Jeremy," I whispered to my husband, "that woman keeps staring at us!" "I know," Jeremy said, "but just act natural." He knew better than to tell me to "act natural," as if that is actually something I'm capable of accomplishing. I tried! I really did and nearly succeeded, except for continually stealing glances at her only to find her still staring at us. We overhead the barista ask, "What can I get started for you?" to which she replied, "I'm still looking." Looking indeed, she was looking at us!

At that moment she trepidatiously walked over to us and broke the awkward silence. "Excuse me," then stepping closer she said slightly above the tone of a whisper, "Do you have the envelope?" In utter confusion, Jeremy responded with the same words he always uses when his mind is desperately trying to comprehend what is happening but falling short. "I'm sorry?" She said it again, "Do you have the envelope?" I was stunned and just knew we were about to be sucked into some kind of criminal investigation. Jeremy asked, "What envelope?" As if she thought we were bluffing, she pushed the matter further. "I was told to meet you in the church parking lot. When you pulled out, I saw you motion for me to follow you." This explained a lot but took a few seconds to sink in. We hadn't been in a church parking lot since we left Elkhart. Suddenly it hit us. In disbelief and astonishment Jeremy said, "Are you saying you followed us all the way here from Elkhart?" "Yes," she answered, with obvious disappointment falling upon her face. I'm pretty sure my mouth was wide open, but I had no words. Jeremy kindly said, "Ma'am, I am very sorry. I don't know what you saw, but I never motioned for you to follow me. I didn't even see you in the Elkhart church parking lot. I noticed you only once we arrived here in Goshen. I am terribly sorry if you thought I was somebody else." She stood there for a minute as if the air had been let out of her sails, yet still convinced that we were bluffing, waiting for us to pull out the coveted envelope from our coat pocket. "You don't have an envelope for me?" she asked again, to which we said "No." Finally she blurted out, "I need a job, okay!" With even more confusion, we apologized, and she stood there trying to process how all of this went wrong. "I'm sorry you followed us so far away from Elkhart. Can I buy you a coffee?" Jeremy offered. She almost scoffed, "I don't need the calories." And on that note she walked out the door. Jeremy and I stood there and looked at each other, unsure of what to do and how to proceed with our day. It was comical in one sense but extremely strange. We were not fearful at all but couldn't help but feel a little violated just knowing that we had been watched and followed for about thirty minutes. The barista looked up at us and curiously asked, "Do you know her?" We told her that we had no idea who that lady was and she said what everyone in ear shot was thinking, "How strange!"

Getting back into our car, Jeremy and I both expressed how strange of an experience this was. We began to explore scenarios and consider what might've been scheduled to happen in that church parking lot. Was it a drug deal? An illegal purchase of some kind? What was in the supposed envelope? Money? Was the envelope question and confession of losing her job an attempt to play on our emotions? We considered it all, but will never know.

The one thing we did conclude from this strange story was that it sounded like an Adventures In Odyssey episode. It was the identical kind of scenario that Whit, Connie, or Eugene might get caught up in. Jason Whitaker would've chased her down and found out the facts. We let her get away but held onto the story, the strangest thing that had happened so far in our travels.

JOY ON THE JOURNEY

Yes, it is true, I have learned a lesson from a coddiwhomple: There are extreme amounts of joy found within the journey, even before we make it to our destination. Although the destination is ultimate in every way, within each winding mile, the word of God promises a life walking with Him will produce "... joy unspeakable and full of glory"(1 Peter 1:8).

Psalm 16:11 says, "In thy presence is fullness of joy, and at thy right hand are pleasures forever more"! Who said life with God is a life of misery? He daily loads us with benefits! I will tightly hold to the hand of Jesus as I walk this narrow road, for with Him on this journey of life, there is fullness of joy.

I recall one afternoon in our travels, my husband and I were strolling through a store when a wooden sign caught our eye. "All Of This and Heaven Too." It surely sums up a life living for Jesus. On the journey with Him we get all of this joy, all of His peace that passes understanding, and His love that will consistently cast out fear. And to think we get all of this, and heaven, too!

CHAPTER SIX

*the purpose
of the pasture*

My answer has not changed! The mountainous west/northwest United States remains my favorite place to travel. Horses, antelope, sheep, tumbleweeds, and scenic views are everywhere. My eyes are always peering through our windows with adolescent curiosity of what lies ahead when driving through the stunning state of Wyoming. I squeal every time we come over a hill with new mountainous peaks in the distance or see the hundreds of antelope playing on the hills. God seems all the closer to me in the mountains! Watching the wild horses gallop over steep ravines is something I used to only dream of seeing. And yet I was watching it all through the crisp windows of our motorhome. We turned a corner engulfed with mountains and rolling hills on each side. We saw hundreds of white sheep speckling the hills. It was a warm and almost Biblical sight to behold. And then I gasped.

"Jeremy!" My excited shrill tone came through again, "It's a fluffy black sheep!" While hundreds of white sheep safely roamed inside the fence line, there was one black sheep outside the fence, near the road. He was small, covered in black fluffy fur, and absolutely adorable. Yet, he was lost. He was separated from the others. He was not surrounded by the protection of the fence. He had somehow escaped the safety of the pasture. Whether from his own cunning devices or by accidentally meandering through a hole, I do not know. It could be that he was keenly aware of how the others saw him, the outcast, the odd one. Maybe he had felt the stinging glares of those spotless white sheep who claimed to have it all together more than the lone black sheep. Whatever the reason, he was now quite literally the outsider.

As we flew by at sixty-five miles per hour, I saw the fretful outcome and impending danger all too clearly. The sheer cliffs that called his name, yet they would quickly drop him to his death. The tangled bramble and painful thistles that would mangle his beautiful coat. The promise and attraction of wild berries, yet never knowing some of the most beautiful berries contain the most poison. Inside the pasture, there is a shepherd who protects from these things. The shepherd knows the poisonous berry, never allowing it to enter his side of the fence, but this little black sheep had no way of knowing. He was all by himself, relying only on his own strength and instincts to guide him.

I wanted to slam on the breaks and pick him up. I wanted to hold the little guy, perhaps put a blanket around him to make him feel protected and cared for. I could see that he was lost and imagined how lonely he must have felt. All I could feel was the isolation and pain of a rejected heart. With overwhelming compassion consuming me, something happened. In the middle of the Wyoming mountains, I caught a glimpse of God's unconditional love toward us. I understood why our treatment of others who dwell both inside and outside the pasture is so important. We are to be Christ-like. To put it simply, I then understood in a new light why Jesus so willingly left the ninety-nine in order to seek out the one sheep who had gone astray. He did it for me, He's done it for you. Whether we are talking sheep or people, the reality is that we were never created to be self-sustainable. We need more than our strength alone. We are only the creation, not the creator. Why would we think His love for someone else would be any different?

Some chapters are written for the reader, this chapter is written and preserved for me to read over again and again. I desire you, dear reader, to listen in and understand my spirit. I am speaking to me, but let us be changed together.

THE PURPOSE OF THE PASTURE

I have heard the arguments more times than I can count. "A pasture gives the impression that there are fences, and I don't want to be fenced in," they say. "Why would I want to serve a God that restricts my life and keeps me from doing whatever I want? That's control! Are the fences really necessary?"

I have heard it all, the hatred of fences, the disdain for boundaries. In fact, I regretfully remember all too clearly the day two young ladies in a church took me, as a very young girl, outside after church to speak privately to me. As any young girl innocently does, I looked up to them and considered them to be beautiful. Out of earshot from my parents, they began to tell me that nakedness and immodesty was okay and even biblical, reminding me that Eve was naked. Their rebellious spirits used persuasive words in an attempt to convince me, through twisted Scripture and perspective that modesty was unnecessary. Their words seemed to claim that what was taught from the pulpit and practiced in our home was wrong, and even deemed it ridiculous. Being so young, I remember trying to wrap my mind around what they were saying. I struggled to accept that they themselves might actually believe what they had told me, yet their views had been made clear. In their eyes, I was fenced in by my parents' teaching, as if it was their doctrine alone and not the Word of God. In my adolescent years, it was my experience with God that I relied on more than theological study, which I also love. More than anything that can be taught, what I had experienced to be real could not be argued or taken from me. I remember quickly concluding and knowing within my heart that what they were saying was wrong. I knew it was wrong, yet in my childlike mind I had no arsenal of Scripture ready to rattle back and dismantle their accusations. Besides, with their rebellious spirit, there wasn't anything I could say or any Scripture I could quote that would provoke them to repent over all they had said. I just knew, unlike them, that I did not want to leave the pasture. As a young girl still vulnerable and impressionable, I knew I was safe there. I found great joy in going to church and in feeling the Good Shepherd's presence. My father, who was also my pastor, mirrored the loving kindness of God and like a shepherd tended faithfully to the flock that had been entrusted to him. Why would I want to leave this place of refuge? Isaiah foretold of Christ in this beautifully descriptive way:

"He shall feed his flock like a shepherd: he shall gather the lambs with his arm, and carry them in his bosom, and shall gently lead those that are with young."
Isaiah 40:11

Those words, their beauty being their truth, speak of the Shepherd's pasture. There is nourishment and provision within the pasture. We are cared for with gentleness and loving kindness. Why anyone would want to leave the boundaries of the fence?

"The Lord is my shepherd; I shall not want. He maketh me to lie down in green pastures: he leadeth me beside the still waters."
Psalm 23:1

Being near the shepherd and under his watch leaves nothing for want. Why leave the pasture when we lack nothing nor want for anything? His presence itself is as refreshing to the soul as being surrounded by lush greenery and rivers of water. There is incomparable rest within His presence.

"Come now, and let us reason together, saith the LORD: though your sins be as scarlet, they shall be as white as snow; though they be red like crimson, they shall be as wool."
Isaiah 1:18

"Purge me with hyssop, and I shall be clean: wash me, and I shall be whiter than snow."
Psalm 51:7

In spite of my many failures and flaws, I know that forgiveness is always found inside the protection of the pasture. As white as the wool of a spotless lamb, our Good Shepherd cleanses the repentant heart and purifies them from sin. How beautiful the thought that

The Purpose of the Pasture

He bids us "come," even after our failures. There is no rejection found within our Savior. When I fail to follow His leading, He never separates himself from me. When I wander too far from His voice, He never turns away His gaze. When I longingly look to other fields and wonder if there's a better way, He never banishes me from His presence nor puts me out to a pasture of less promise. When I confess my faults, there is no condemnation found in Him. He pulls me close to His side and covers me in grace. Why would I want to leave a pasture like that?

> *"Thou preparest a table before me in the presence of mine enemies: thou anointest my head with oil; my cup runneth over. Surely goodness and mercy shall follow me all the days of my life: and I will dwell in the house of the LORD for ever."*
> *Psalm 23:5-6*

When thistles have matted my coat and I have made a mess of things, inside the pasture I can run into His safe embrace. Sure, there will always be unavoidable enemies even within the pasture, yet the enemy shall never triumph as long as I continue to follow the shepherd and partake of what He has provided. From even our most aggressive adversary, He is our shield. That, alone, is reason enough to stay in the pasture!

Our Shepherd is not one to run from; His loving kindness draws us toward Himself. Once a heart has experienced the unconditional love of the Shepherd, they understand more profoundly David's invitation: "O taste and see that the LORD is good" (Psalm 34:8). Among all of David's poetic writings and musical compositions which describe the greatness of God, his thirty-fourth Psalm invites the listener to go beyond believing his own description. He challenges us to experience Him for ourselves, to "taste and see."

His pasture is where I belong. I am happy. I am free. I have joy within the deepest part of my heart. Others may come and go, sheep may wander from the fold and forsake the Shepherd's call, but I will keep my eyes upon Him and my ear tuned to hear His voice.

Fences? Oh yes, I am happy to say there are fences. My flesh is drawn to evil and so easily lured by sin. The clear-cut boundary of the fence keeps me from chasing down things that are purposed to destroy me. The fence not only keeps me in and keeps me protected from my own self, but it also keeps the enemy out. It stands between the abundant life that God desires for me and my own selfish demise. The fence secures me from the roaring lion who walketh about, seeking whom he may devour (1 Peter 5:8). The fence is that standard which rises up in the face of the enemy, clearly defining how far away he must stay from the sheep who are safe within the arms of the Shepherd.

To interpret the fences as being offensive and unnecessary is to lack understanding of the one keeping us safe. "For God so loved the world, that he gave..." (John 3:16). He gave His life in demonstration of His great love toward us. Not that we would be restricted in life but that we might be free from sin and the curse that it brings. Simply put, true freedom is found within the fence!

I haven't changed my mind after all these years. I'm older now, but my feelings today are the same as when I stood on the church steps and heard those beautiful girls who I desired to be godly, spew out such ungodliness. I still don't want to leave the protection of the pasture. I am still thankful for fences. I still love the unspeakable joy that is unique to the flock of God. His anointing is still precious to me. My cup still "runneth over." I suppose that if anything has changed at all, it is my passion to welcome others into this glorious pasture with loving, open arms like the Shepherd.

A HIGH PRICED COAT

We are all probably familiar with the term, "black sheep." We use that label to describe a disreputable member of a group, especially within a family. They are the outcasts, the oddballs, the ones outside the family fence.

This term was derived long ago. The wool of a black sheep has traditionally been considered to be of lesser value than that of a white lamb. The commercial market claims that no one wanted black wool, and it was too difficult to die black wool and make it white, therefore it was deemed invaluable. Only the meat of a black sheep was sold. In other words, they were only good for anything once they were dead. A shepherd in Augusta Springs, Virginia, explained, "A black sheep was really one you just got rid of." It was undesirable. It held lesser value to the shepherd and was looked down upon by everyone.

But our Shepherd is not like other shepherds. Jesus Christ made Himself as one of us so that we might become like Him. He allowed His seamless white coat, which symbolizes His righteousness and holiness, to be taken from Him on Calvary so that you and I, whose lives had been blackened by the curse, could exchange our heavy sin-darkened garment for a garment

114

of righteousness. The Bible tells that the soldiers who had beaten, blasphemed, and bound Christ to the cross with nails, gambled for His seamless coat so that it would not be rent in pieces. It seems painful and inappropriate by our standards that one of those cruel men would receive the coat of Christ. Of all the injustices that we see sewn into the fabric of Calvary's scene, it is this occurrence that has made me most frustrated. Why didn't Mary, who birthed and raised Him and endured the agony of watching Him die, inherit the coat of her son? She could have clutched it tight and held it close, letting the fabric muffle her moans and cries. That garment, which she had often seen lay on the back of her Son, might have shown a ray of light into her dark grief had it been placed in her possession. Since this grieving mother could no longer look upon Him, how comforting it would have been for her to look upon the coat that He wore and remember the life that He lived.

If not Mary, why not John? That faithful and beloved disciple who followed Christ to His cross was certainly a worthy candidate to take home the Master's coat. The others had scattered and forsaken Him, yet John seemed to trust Jesus with what he did not understand and was there to console Mary at the foot of the cross when Jesus took His last breath. That alone, in and of itself, seems worthy of reward. In John there seems to be no wavering, no compromise, no disavowing of devotion: only loyalty and commitment. John would've forever cherished the coat of Christ had it been willed to him and placed in his care. Didn't he deserve it?

By our standards, the coat should've been given to Mary or John, yet we must be reminded that what Christ came to do and offer unto humanity has never been predicated on our worth or anything we can do to qualify ourselves for His grace. The righteousness of God isn't rewarded to us according to our goodness. Though I once thought it strange that the coat would be placed into the hands of those Roman soldiers, I now see it for the beauty it is. Sinful and evil men who watched Christ died. If they didn't have a chance at his coat, neither would I. Calvary's one purpose was to make the righteousness of God accessible to every man by the conquering of death and the defeating of sin's curse.

"For all have sinned, and come short of the glory of God"
Romans 3:23

"I will greatly rejoice in the LORD, my soul shall be joyful in my God; for he hath clothed me with the garments of salvation, he hath covered me with the robe of righteousness..."
Isaiah 61:10

Our righteousness is as filthy rags, yet we can now be clothed in the righteousness of Christ. Our black coat can be exchanged for one whiter than snow. The exchange is unfair by all accounts, yet that is the great depth of God's love toward us.

Contrary to the old shepherd's rejection of the black sheep and its wool, something has changed in our culture. Now the tables have turned and black sheep are just as valuable as the white ones. Dark wool is no longer disdained, but it is in high demand in the fashion industry. "Black sheep are great," a fashion designer in New York said. "I take the black wool and mix it with white wool and make beautiful yarn from it: light gray, medium gray, dark gray, light tweed, medium tweed, and dark tweed. You don't have to dye it and you can make beautiful garments from black wool." Because of the growing demand for black wool in New York City's garment district, a man named Chester has a black ram and is building up his flock of black sheep to meet the need.

What was once the very least is now considered the very best, all because someone saw the value of the black sheep and chose not to waste the wool. Shepherds of old might've thought black wool wasn't worth their time, but I thank God that the Good Shepherd always takes time for the black sheep. For those who repent of their sins, are baptized in Jesus' name, and receive the precious gift of the Holy Ghost, we have the promise that "He is faithful and just to forgive us our sins, and to cleanse us from all unrighteousness" (1 John 1:9).

> "Come now, and let us reason together, saith the LORD: though your sins be as scarlet, they shall be as white as snow; though they be red like crimson, they shall be as wool."
> Isaiah 1:18

FRIENDSHIP WITH THE GOOD SHEPHERD

The Shepherd desires to know us and call us friends. How wonderful Abraham must have been. I have almost been envious of Abraham at times, thinking of his God-given title, "a friend of God." Surely with a title like that, there was something special about Abraham, almost unattainable by us. And yet, we find within a few pages of his story, he was an imperfect human

117

just like you and me. He lied. Oh, how he lied. And even to this sinner, God gives the warm invitation of friendship.

Friendship doesn't demand perfection, it requires repentance. The truth is Abraham was a friend of God because he understood that a relationship with God requires daily worship and a daily walk with the Lord. When Abraham sinned, he found an altar. He didn't tuck his tail and run away from God in those moments of disobedience. He, through friendship, understood that God alone is able and willing to forgive, therefore Abraham never failed to keep an open line of communication with God.

Closeness in friendship is always nested upon honest, vulnerable, and open communication. I remember desperately wanting to befriend a young lady whom I knew to be struggling. To my disappointment, no matter how hard I tried to reach out and encourage her, she only pulled away and avoided me all the more. I invited her out for coffee on numerous occasions and even desired to spoil her at the fanciest of bakeries, yet she would only retreat from every invitation. In frustration, I remember telling Jeremy, "It is impossible to help someone and be a blessing to them when they simply won't receive it." The frustration dissipated as soon as I realized that is how God feels towards us when we avoid Him and shun His ever faithful invitations. He desires to bless, comfort, and direct our steps, yet He can do nothing of benefit to us unless we allow Him access to our life. Even an all powerful God cannot have relationship with one who rejects Him.

A LOST SHEEP AND A PRODIGAL BROTHER

Although there are multiple emotions woven within the story of the prodigal son, when I imagine the father seeing his son return and running to welcome him home, there is an exceptionally powerful emotion that wells up within me. This alone encapsulates how far and forgiving our own heavenly Father is toward those wayward souls who wander out from under His protection and promise. The faithfulness of the father to continually look down the lane, hoping to see the silhouette of his son, reveals the greatest desire and deepest longing of God. He delights in the repentance of His children. He longs to restore unto us what sin separated us from. He freely gives forgiveness unto those who will humble themselves before Him, acknowledging the err of their ways and giving themselves in servitude.

Before the returned prodigal could finish pouring out his heart and repenting for his foolish ways—probably a speech he had rehearsed many times along the long journey home—the father interrupted him with joy and love. With arms flung tightly around his son, and tears of joy drenching his face, forgiveness was granted without the bat of an eye. This was the moment for which this father had anxiously waited. How could he not rejoice? How could he not lavish the lad with forgiveness and grace? Mirrored in the actions of this father, we see the heartbeat of God. For every prodigal that has walked away, God is faithfully watching. There isn't a repentant prayer prayed that doesn't put a smile on His face. There isn't a sinner who kneels at the altar of consecration and turns from his sin who doesn't make heaven happy. Jesus said, "Joy shall be in heaven over one

119

sinner that repenteth," (Luke 15:7). What a moment it must be in heaven when the celebration of a soul forgiven begins. What a celebration that must've took place in the street as the father and his son were reunited again.

We must be reminded that our Father is consumed with a heart for the lost. He longs to see every sinner forgiven, every wayward soul restored, and every heart made new. There isn't a son or daughter who God has given up on and no longer desires to see return unto Himself. Our heavenly Father ever continually looks down the long and winding road of life, hoping to lavish upon another soul the gift of forgiveness. If that is His desire, it must be ours also. We must not become so busy in the field that we forsake to know Him and accompany Him in His mission to welcome the weary and love the lost.

The older brother missed it. While working in the field for his father and furthering his father's kingdom, the older brother had failed to truly know the heart of his father. It seems that he cared not for those outside the kingdom. How easy it can be to be a part of Kingdom things and yet have no real relationship with the Father. It's possible to labor faithfully in our field, yet never know what truly moves the heart of the one we serve. If that older brother had been close to his dad, he would have known how desperately he desired to see his lost son come home. If the older brother had spent more time with his father, he would have known his father's dreams and desires. He would have understood the wrinkles of worry that weathered his father's face. He would've heard his father speak of the lost and envision his return. He would've joined his father in daily looking down the driveway, lest his father be left to look alone. The son who stayed would have heard it said, "If he ever comes home, I will welcome him as though he never left. I will honor him. I will rejoice. I just want my son home safely." He should have known that his father could never be content with ninety-nine in the fold as long as there was one little black sheep outside the safety and protection of the fence.

When the sounds of celebration had filled the air and drifted out into the far reaches of the field where the older brother toiled, he was so disconnected that he couldn't imagine what might be happening. Uncomfortable to enter the father's house and uneasy at anyone's party but his own, he asked a servant what the cause for this celebration might be. Upon hearing that his brother had returned, this brother was infuriated by the thought that a sinner could be celebrated above himself who had remained faithful and never forsook his father's kingdom. And yet it is amazing to me that the father demonstrated the same consistent love toward the older son as he had the younger son by meeting his older son outside. When he refused to enter into the father's house, the father met him on the outside. Oh, how he pleaded for his son to join in the celebration because there is great blessing found in the celebrating of others. When words of exposed bitterness and offense had been spoken, the father quietly replied to his son, "Everything I have is yours. But we had to celebrate and be glad, because this brother of yours was dead and is alive again; he was lost and is found," (Luke 15:31-32 NIV).

Under the cover of night, in direct contrast to the light shining through the windows of jubilee inside the father's house, it is clear to see who the lost soul was that evening. Jesus, in telling this parable, was speaking straight to the Pharisees and left it open ended and haunting. Spiritual they claimed to be, yet, clothed in their own garments of self righteousness and judgment toward others, they failed to see that they were the lost sheep in need of a Savior.

I must confess that I can recall times in my own life when ignorant to my doings and clothed in my own robe of self righteousness, I have treated others the same way. To the black sheep who wasn't like me, to those who I deemed to be beneath my level of spirituality, to the person I looked down upon and judged, I shudder to think how harshly I might've dealt with them. I cringe to think of the times in which I, in my ignorance, have made others feel inferior to me. If God could love me, shouldn't I love them? If He could forgive my sins, how could I hold another accountable for theirs? I am moved to repentance when I consider how many times my actions may have taken on the form of a Pharisee instead of mirroring the love of the Good Shepherd. "I want to be like the master," I say so often, yet I fall short of that desire every time I misjudge a wounded heart. Sheep who cast judgment and cause pain are no reflection of our Shepherd.

My mind races back to that little black sheep in Wyoming. How easily we could make a sheep within a pasture feel uncomfortable and unwelcome. If they do not feel accepted within the pasture, of course they will find a way out! We must see them as Christ sees them, valuable and precious no matter their appearance or past. We, the sheep who stay inside the pasture, must never fall into the trap of frustration when the Shepherd leaves us to search for the one that is in danger. There ought to be excitement within ourselves to know that the lost is being found, the wayward is being rescued.

We, who have been cleansed and made white, should delight in knowing that another is coming into the safety of the pasture.

So often in Scripture we read these words, "Jesus looked upon them and had compassion on them." It leads me to conclude that where there is compassion, there is no room for judgment. I know it sounds silly, but when seeing the black sheep outside the fence, I never thought "How dare he not be in the pasture!" All I felt was compassion and the urgency to protect him from waiting danger. That must always be our response when seeing the lost souls of our world living beneath their privilege, outside the protection of God's pasture. May our souls be moved with compassion. Yes, it took a black sheep in Wyoming to teach me this truth, but there are black sheep right here in my life, within my reach, that must be saved and brought into the protection of the pasture. God, help me to show them the purpose of the pasture.

THE VOICE OF THE SHEPHERD

There are times when I find myself wishing I could've been present amid the amazing happening of which I read in the Bible. I can almost picture myself in the crowd. The story that is told in the tenth chapter of John is just one of the instances. The eye of my mind imagines people perched in a grassy garden with daisies and wild flowers springing up in between the rocks. I can see the Pharisees standing on the outskirts, close enough to hear, yet far enough away to make a statement. I see pretty women, happy children, strong men, and young, growing boys numbered among the crowd that intently listens to what Jesus has to say. His words left the Pharisees with audacious outcries of fury, yet His simple,

The Purpose of the Pasture

kind, and confident truths continually drew the crowds to His feet. In His words we see the way of our Shepherd.

"My sheep hear my voice, and I know them, and they follow me: And I give unto them eternal life; and they shall never perish, neither shall any man pluck them out of my hand."
John 10:27

As I read those words, I realized that I have no need to be envious of the crowds of that day. He is as near unto me as He was unto them. His Words are just as true today as they were in the days of His earthly ministry. His comfort and peace is as real now as it ever was. His mission is toward us as it was toward them: to give eternal life. Just as they did, I, too, know His voice. I, too, follow where He leads. I, too, have found Him to be wonderful and worthy. I, too, have settled it in my soul: I trust the Good Shepherd. Now I can show others how wonderful He is.

The first prayer recorded in the Bible is Abraham's prayer, and it was a selfless prayer for others. Abraham surely did know the heartbeat of God through friendship with Him! I pray I will never lose sight of the heart of my Shepherd, knowing we, also, must reach and rejoice for the one who has been away from the ninety-nine. It is always about the lost.

"The thief cometh not, but for to steal, and to kill, and to destroy: I am come that they might have life, and that they might have it more abundantly. I am the good shepherd: the good shepherd giveth his life for the sheep."
John 10:10-11

CHAPTER SEVEN

a handful
of blackberries
part one

"Oh Jamin, that's not big enough." Those were the words of my oldest sister as she stared at the large, twenty-four ounce cup I held in my hand. It then dawned on me that she and I had very different ideas in mind when we decided to leisurely pick blackberries together.

There we sat in a small town, bored out of our minds, with nowhere to go and nothing to do. The world around us was shut down due to the global pandemic. After exhausting our baking abilities, becoming bored with card games, and walking for miles until our bodies were sore, it seemed like the only thing left to do in Daisetta, Texas, was to pick blackberries. It was her idea, not mine. The sun was shining bright and burning hot on a typical humid Texas day. The motorhome was struggling to keep cool, and with the options of activities running thin, I reluctantly agreed. I never do well sitting around, after all. She disappeared and soon returned with a large bucket big enough to feed blackberries for the whole town. We jumped on my uncle's golf cart and meandered our way to the place where the berries grew.

My sister and I are very different. I was finished after the first two handfuls, yet she was determined to fill up that large bucket. Full of frustration and nearly suffering from a heat stroke, I croaked,

A Handful of Blackberries: Part One

"How are we ever going to fill this bucket?" Never looking away from the berries that were within her grasp, my sister said, "One handful at a time."

How could I argue with such a simple, yet profound, truth? I continued on. Each singular blackberry I picked soon turned into a handful. After that handful came another. Somehow, without fainting from the humid heat, we managed to fill up the bucket and still remain both sisters and friends. For the next several hours and days, that bucket of blackberries served as the source of much enjoyment. My sister took to the kitchen and made blackberry jam and brownies with blackberry butter cream frosting. Tasting the sweet and delicious product of our labor suddenly made the hard work and energy spent seem worth it. It took time, but every handful played a part in the finished product.

A LITTLE HANDFUL

It can be easy to fall prey to the mindset that says a handful isn't enough, a small amount, a simple thing cannot make a difference. In 2 Kings chapter five, Naaman was angered and refused to perform the simple task that was given him by the prophet Elisha.

"And Elisha sent a messenger unto him, saying, Go and wash in Jordan seven times, and thy flesh shall come again to thee, and thou shall be clean."
2 Kings 5:10

The instructions were simple, and the outcome was clear, yet to Naaman it seemed too simple and insignificant to bring about a miraculous healing. A servant reminded him that had the prophet required him to do some great thing, then he would've gladly followed the prophet's direction. The blunt honesty of that servant revealed Naaman's failure but also ours. We too are guilty of doubting the effects that small things can make. We struggle to believe that something as simple as a little obedience and a handful of faith can open the door for the miraculous. Simple, daily decisions that seem so small have the ability to make an eternal difference.

"For who hath despised the day of small things?"
Zechariah 4:10

Only a handful of brave men made up Gideon's army and, with God, they won the victory. The feeding of the five thousand men, plus women and children, was possible because of a boy who gave a handful of fish and bread to the Master. The widow of Zeraphath had only a handful of meal and a small measure of oil, yet she did as the prophet instructed and never exhausted her supply. The examples are many that prove this principle to be true. What seems like only an insignificant handful to us is more than enough for God to take and do something great.

PETER'S PRACTICAL INSTRUCTION

The life and ministry of Peter is fascinating to me because of his rash and radical personality. I am continually amazed at how temperamental he could be, yet how powerfully anointed and used of God he was. In his younger years Peter most likely was not known for his practicality or methodical approaches. He was widely known for his impulsiveness and spontaneity, yet the Apostle matured and grew in grace over the years. By the time that Peter penned his second epistle, he had perhaps settled some of his sporadic and spontaneous habits and learned that some things require instruction, intentionality, and faithfulness. In the opening verses of his letter, Peter conveys some simple and practical concepts that should be carefully and strategically added to our lives on a daily basis.

> *"Whereby are given unto us exceeding great and precious promises: that by these ye might be partakers of the divine nature, having escaped the corruption that is in the world through lust. And beside this, giving all diligence, add to your faith virtue; and to virtue knowledge; And to knowledge temperance; and to temperance patience; and to patience godliness; And to godliness brotherly kindness; and to brotherly kindness charity. For if these things be in you, and abound, they make you that ye shall neither be barren nor unfruitful in the knowledge of our Lord Jesus Christ. But he that lacketh these things is blind, and cannot see afar off, and hath forgotten that he was purged from his old sins. Wherefore the rather, brethren, give diligence to make your calling and election sure: for if ye do these things, ye shall never fall:"*
> *2 Peter 1:4-10*

The beauty of these instructions is that they are accompanied and concluded with the motivating promise that "If ye do these things, ye shall never fall." There is a plurality of things that must be done to guard oneself. A handful of faith alone is not enough. Virtue, knowledge, or temperance by themselves are not sufficient.

Any one thing we add to our lives will never be enough to keep us. We need a handful of this and a handful of that. The big bucket would have never been filled had I stopped with my first handful of blackberries. It took many handfuls to fill the bucket. There were moments when I was tired and ready to quit, yet I continued to add another handful to the bucket. Likewise, it takes many handfuls in our spiritual walk with God.

Peter gave us practical instructions to avoid failure and backsliding. Any God-fearing believer should be gripped by this passage and study it fervently so that she can intentionally do everything within her power to please the Lord. Let's look at these eight "handfuls" together.

FAITH

Faith, of course, must be first. There is no beginning without faith. Faith is the foundation upon which everything else in our walk with God stands. Faith is the anchor of every believer and the missing piece within the heart of the unbeliever. A man without faith can rely on nothing more than his own strength, yet the child of God, who is full of faith, can lean upon the strength and power of God.

> *"But without faith it is impossible to please him: for he that cometh to God must believe that he is, and that he is a rewarder of them that diligently seek him."*
> *Hebrews 11:6*

The truth is we all have faith. Paul told the Romans that, "God hath dealt to every man the measure of faith" (Romans 12:3). Some simply choose to place their faith in things other than God. We exercise extreme amounts of faith every time we place an order, drive a car, or walk across the street; therefore, it is not a question of whether or not we possess faith. The question is this: What have we put our faith in?

The writer of Hebrews clearly stated that it takes faith in order to believe that God exists. It takes faith in God's Word to believe "In the beginning God created the heaven and the earth" (Genesis 1:1). "Through faith we understand that the worlds were framed by the word of God" (Hebrews 11:3). Yet through archeology, science, and documented history there is an enormous amount of evidence that proves the validity and truth of the Word of God. It takes more faith to doubt the Bible than it does to believe it is true. The amount of faith required to believe that there was an uncaused explosion which brought everything intricately into existence is incalculable. I choose to believe and place all of my faith in the Word of God!

"Now faith is the substance of things hoped for, the evidence of things not seen. For by it the elders obtained a good report."
Hebrews 11:1-2

I dare not believe that there is even one Christian who hasn't at some point asked themselves the question: Do I have enough faith to endure until the end? That wondering is a natural instinct that will inevitably come to the surface at times. Should our faith be dead and dormant, then we are right in questioning our spiritual survival and endurance, yet if our faith is continually growing and ever expanding, we can be assured that our faith is enough to carry us. Rather than asking, "Do I have enough faith," we would do better to ask, "Is my faith growing?"

"But I have prayed for thee, that thy faith fail not: and when thou art converted, strengthen thy brethren"
Luke 22:32

Perhaps the remembrance of that very statement, spoken by his Lord, is what made Peter so passionate to pass on the practical instructions that we read in 2 Peter 1. Faith, in its mere existence, is not enough. Faith must be growing, lest it fails. Faith must be added to, lest it falters. The same prayer that Jesus prayed over Peter reaches into our day and is also the desire of God toward us. There may be failures along the way, but each of us have the ability and opportunity to finish strong in our faith. Our faith must not fail!

"Looking into Jesus, the author and finished of our faith."
Hebrews 12:2

I suppose the most prominent figure of faith in Scripture is Abraham, the father of the faithful who "staggered not at the promise of God through unbelief; but was strong in faith, giving glory to God; And being fully persuaded that, what he had promised, he was able also to perform" (Romans 4:20-21).

"by faith Abraham, when he was called to go into a place which he should after receive for an inheritance, obeyed; and he went out,

not knowing wither he went. By faith he sojourned in the land of promise, as in a strange country, dwelling in tabernacles with Issac and Jacob, the hero's with him of the same promise: for he looked for a city which hath foundations, whose builder and maker was God."
Hebrews 11:9

Abraham was not content to dwell in a land without a sure foundation of faith. Ur of the Chaldees had become evil and full of idol worship; therefore, God said, "Get thee out of thy country, and from thy kindred, and from thy father's house, unto a land that I will shew thee" (Genesis 12:1). Abraham could no longer live there and preserve or progress his faith in God. In an environment of sin, faith in God would die. Sure, he could have chosen to remain in Ur of the Chaldees and enjoy the comfort and security of being settled, but he had to forsake his place of comfort in exchange for a pursuit of greater faith. Perhaps sleeping on the ground at times, and longing for the comforts of his old home-place, Abraham insistently refused to give up and return to the evil land which God had called him out of. Though every step required more faith, Abraham knew that the fulfilled promise of God would prove to be worth every ounce of uncertainty and trust. The world calls our faith in God foolish, yet the truth remains that we can have no spiritual foundation in an environment of wickedness and evil. Faith may take us on a journey of growth, but it will always be worth it.

Abraham became known for his faith. There were times that he doubted and failed to believe, yet it seemed as though faith always won out in the end. Even the Philistine King in Genesis 21:22 took notice and said of Abraham, "God is with thee in all that thou doest." The world is not blind, nor do they fail to notice the child of God that is truly filled with faith. Our faith in God must not be hidden away or tucked out of sight. Faith must be before all. Faith must be over all.

With faith like unto that of Abraham, we are able to affect others beyond ourselves. The spiritual blessings that you and I enjoy today are directly connected to the faithfulness and God-fearing lifestyle of Abraham.

"Know ye therefore that they which are of faith, the same are the children of Abraham."
Galatians 3:7

"And if ye be Christ's, then are ye Abraham's seed, and heirs according to the promise."
Galatians 3:29

If we really understood the far reaching effects of our faith, how it brings strength to future generations and effects the faith of others around us, we would not waver as much as we sometimes do. We wouldn't allow our faith to so easily falter. We wouldn't so quickly throw in the towel at times when uncertainty is all we can see. We must always remember that someone tomorrow will be effected by our faith today; therefore, we must let our love and concern for those who will follow us bring strength to our own discipline.

Spanning twenty-eight verses, the writer of Hebrews walks his reader down the hallway of the hero's of faith, mentioning name after name and the faith they possessed. It's as if the writer runs out of time and feels the need to hasten on in his letter, not to belabor the point. To transition from chapter eleven to chapter twelve, changing the focus from the faith of others to our own faith, the writer says this:

> *"And what shall I more say? for the time would fail me to tell of Gedeon, and of Barak, and of Samson, and of Jephthae; of David also, and Samuel, and of the prophets: Who through faith subdued kingdoms, wrought righteousness, obtained promises, stopped the mouths of lions, Quenched the violence of fire, escaped the edge of the sword, out of weakness were made strong, waxed valiant in fight..."*
> Hebrews 11:32-34

While I enjoy studying the life stories of each name that is listed in Hebrews chapter eleven, I take more away from that chapter than simply an expanded knowledge of Bible patriarchs. I have concluded that the faith of the faithful is powerful and far-reaching. As did their faith, so can your faith conquer kingdoms, bring forth righteousness, obtain promises, shut the mouths of lions, quench the violence of fire, escape the edge of the sword, bring forth strength in weakness, and become mighty in war. That is what faith can do!

To pray in faith unto the Lord each day can seem a small thing indeed. To consistently set aside time to read God's Word can seem routine and ritualistic at times, but without daily hiding His Word in our hearts we have no arsenal of defense against sin. It is impossible to fight our adversary without exercising obedience to God's Word.

There, within its pages, we find promises and truths upon which we firmly stand and draw strength from. Some will laugh at my love for God and my faithfulness in serving Him, yet I will continue on. Though my devotion seem small, insignificant, and like unto only a handful to some, I know that every small action of faith is accumulated and contributes daily to my salvation. I choose faith over all!

VIRTUE

"Who can find a virtuous woman? For her price is far beyond rubies."
Proverbs 31:10

How often have I read that chapter of the Bible. When my husband and I were engaged to be married, we shared with each other a list that each of us had written years before, describing what we desired in our future spouse. I had forgotten all about my list, yet when I found it, my mind was blown when I realized that Jeremy not only matched every detailed description of the man I desired, he exceeded them. Jeremy had a list also, written on a piece of paper from a hotel room notepad. He listed the things he wanted and didn't want in the woman he would marry. At the bottom of a very detailed and specific list, the last thing he mentioned seemed to sum up every other expectation: "the perfect reflection of a Proverbs 31 woman."

Although I dare not imagine myself to be perfect, I find it beautiful my husband desired a godly woman. I believe every woman can look at the life described in this passage and learn much about the virtuous women that she should continually strive to be. A virtuous woman is a hard worker, clothed in strength and honor, fearing the Lord at all times. Goodness and kindness come from her lips, and all who speak of her can relate her character with no better descriptive terms than goodness and kindness. There is effortlessly beauty that accompanies goodness.

Virtue is defined, in its essence, as morality and genuine goodness. We know God to be good; therefore, in our pursuit to be like him, we should continually strive to attain goodness. The Bible teaches us that it is His goodness that draws us to repentance. Being made in His image and fashioned according to His likeness, we should be no different. Our goodness, the goodness of God expressed through us, should draw others to Jesus Christ. The world knows morality, and they know what is immoral. Although they often try to justify their immoral actions and sinful lifestyles, they never lose the conscious awareness of what true morality is. A sinner who is not in covenant with God may speak of their wrongs as if they are right, yet a sinner will notice the hypocrisy of a Christian who claims to live like Christ but lives a lifestyle of sin no different than their own. The faithless and immoral may protest righteousness and fight against its presence among them, but they cannot deny it. While a person not in covenant relationship with God may belittle and disregard godliness, wanting to be accepted in their sin, they have nothing but disrespect for those who blur the lines of holiness and partake of sin while professing their salvation. The heart far from God knows the saint should not live as they live.

A practical and biblical key to living a virtuous life is given in Proverbs 16.

"Commit thy works unto the LORD, and thy thoughts shall be established."
Proverbs 16:3

Most of us, myself included, are guilty of trying to get our thoughts under subjection without first subjecting our actions and habits unto the Lord. If we try to conquer our mind and expect our actions to follow suit, we will be left with frustration and failure. We can't always control every thought that enters our mind. Paul told the Corinthian church in his second letter that we do not war after the flesh, but in the Spirit by "casting down imaginations, and every high thing that exalteth itself against the knowledge of God, and bringing into captivity every thought to the obedience of Christ" (2 Corinthians 10:5). Evil thoughts will come to our minds, but we have the ability through Christ to take those thoughts captive and never let them rule our actions. Although we can't control every thought that comes into our mind, we can control our actions. Every child of God must decide to live, move, and breathe in Christ Jesus. By setting forth a standard of godliness in our actions, we are then able to put on the mind of Christ.

Frank W. Boreham said it well when he wrote, "We make our decisions, then our decisions turn around and make us." When our actions lead us to watch immorality in a show or read a story that celebrates ungodly things, those actions plant seeds in our minds that will always produce immoral thoughts. Entertaining evil is not as harmless as some say. When we allow ourselves to watch sin and be entertained by immorality, we are welcoming that into our lives and slowly, but surely, we lose any power that we might have once held over it. Eventually we will do what we have seen done. Our actions will be as the actions of those who we allowed to influence us. The more we allow ourselves to listen and watch things that are contrary to the teaching of Scripture, the harder it is to hear the voice of the Holy Ghost. That teaching voice of the Spirit becomes drowned out and covered up by the ever increasing noise of distraction. We are born sinners and drawn to sin; therefore, it is only natural for us to desire and crave world things when they are placed within our reach. For that reason, I have chosen to separate myself from sin, reject the things of this world, and put only in my reach those things that will drawn me closer to the Lord. His Word is always within my reach. His presence is always what I desire. His Spirit is always my guide. His voice is always what I am listening for. Those things are what I desire and delight in. I have learned that when godliness becomes our comfort zone, what we choose in times of rest will become our source of strength in times of trial. Yes, it is so easy in our culture to become desensitized by sin and ungodliness, yet we must not bow our knees at the altars of pleasure, humor, or entertainment. We must bow only at the feet of Jesus and worship Him alone. If we fall in love with God and long to stand in His presence without blemish, our actions will always seek to honor Him, and His Spirit will steer us away from anything that would separate us from Him. When we dwell upon goodness and mercy, we are no more consumed by a desire for the things of this world. We then desire and earnestly long for the good things of God that are filled with righteousness, peace, and joy in the Holy Ghost. Soon, evil loses its hold, and sin fails to prevail because we have committed our works to God, and God establishes our thoughts.

"Finally, brethren, whatsoever things are true, whatsoever things are honest, whatsoever things are just, whatsoever things are pure, whatsoever things are lovely, whatsoever things are of good report; if there be any virtue, and if there be any praise, think on these things."
Philippians 4:8

I have put this principle to practice in my life and what a difference it makes. When I have scrolled through social media too long and allowed my mind to be bombarded with images and agendas, my mind becomes fixed on those things my eyes have beheld. Yet, the more I think about the Lord, listen to preaching, turn on an uplifting podcast, or engage in a godly conversation, the more spiritually sensitive and biblically conscious I become. The more I listen to music that brings glory to God throughout the day, the more I find myself drawn to worship. My intentional actions put me in a godly frame of mind.

Daily I tell myself, "I will delight only in things which are of good report." It seems like a small, menial task, to daily commit our works, actions, and choices to the Lord, but what an impact that little decision will make. It's just a handful of blackberries each day, yet every handful keeps us from falling.

KNOWLEDGE

The Lord God spoke to the children of Israel through the Prophet Hosea saying,

"My people are destroyed for lack of knowledge: because thou hast

rejected knowledge, I will also reject thee, that thou shalt be no
priest to me: seeing thou hast forgotten the law of thy God, I will
also forget thy children."
Hosea 4:6

It becomes apparent that God has placed a high value upon knowledge and desires that we acquire it lest we be destroyed. Wise Solomon has this to say about wisdom and knowledge:

"Wisdom is the principal thing; therefore get wisdom: and with all
thy getting get understanding"
Proverbs 4:7

Knowledge is another necessary handful that we must daily acquire in order to avoid failure. Paul wrote to the Corinthians concerning the gift of knowledge, which is given by God and associated with the ability to teach and instruct, yet also with forms of revelation similar to prophecy. The most practical form of acquiring knowledge is through the study of Scripture. Many have read the Bible, even in its entirety, yet failed to truly understand and acquire knowledge of what they read. The pursuit of biblical knowledge takes us deeper than merely reading black and red words on a white page. There must be a spiritual element involved in order for the eyes of your understanding to be opened. The power of the Word of God is that it is living and able to reveal truth and insight to those who are hungry and desirous to know and understand the ways of God. Therefore, we must purposely study God's Word until we understand its message and meaning. At that point we receive knowledge and build up an arsenal of understanding that can be used to combat our adversary. When presented with lies, deception, and confusion, we can rely on our knowledge of God's infallible Word to come to our aide and be our defense. No wonder David, being a man after God's own heart, was so strong and vocal in his belief of this practice and its essentiality in his life.

"Thy word have I hid in my heart, that I might not sin against thee."
Psalm 119:11

No one can argue that having a deep respect for Who He is and the grandeur of this majesty is the source from which we obtain resistance against sin. We are able to combat temptation and sin with the Word of God. When Jesus was tempted of the devil in the wilderness following his baptism by John the Baptizer, Jesus responded to every temptation by saying, "It is written." He did not defend himself with human intellect, reasoning, or observation. He did not allow Himself even a moment of time to accept this lie as truth. That should be the place of knowledge and understanding that you and I strive to attain. When we are confronted to the lies and temptations of the enemy, may there be a spring of scriptural substance that flows forth from us. May we always depend upon the law and commandments of God to combat the attack of Satan. Just as Jesus spoke Scripture in the face of Satan, so will I hide the Word of God in my heart that I might be able to boldly declare it with confidence at all times. In doing so, we will always triumph because Satan cannot stand or prevail against the power of the Word. Though Satan is called "the father of lies" in John 8:44, he is not "the everlasting Father" as is Jesus described in Isaiah 9:6. The Prophet foretold of Christ saying, "Of the increase of his government and peace there shall be no end, upon the throne of David, and upon his kingdom, to order it, and to establish it with judgment and with justice from henceforth even for ever" (Isaiah 9:7). Satan may be the lord of the lie, but Jesus is the Lord of all, whose word "is quick, and powerful, and sharper than any two-edged sword, piercing even to the dividing asunder of soul and spirit, and of the joints and marrow, and is a discerner of the thoughts and intents of the heart" (Hebrews 4:12). With a knowledge of His Word, we can defeat confusion and disillusion.

"Study to show thyself approved unto God, a workman that needeth not to be ashamed, rightly dividing the word of truth."
2 Timothy 2:15

Our enemy is immediately defeated when confronted with truth; this is why we must study Scripture for ourselves and let it dwell within us. My mother and father's knowledge of Scripture gives me no power over sin. My grandma and grandpa's deep understanding of truth gives me no authority to combat temptation. I must come to know for myself what they have come to know. I must study and understand in my mind and spirit what they have come to understand. I must study and show myself approved unto God.

Peter understood that a sincere heart can be full of faith and even possess good morals, yet without knowledge of the Word and why we live holy unto God, succumbing to the voices of deception around us becomes easy. When the world asks, "Are these 'rules' that you live by really part of your salvation?" We must have a biblical response. When friends taunt, "It's so much more fun to live however you want. You're missing out!" we must remember that living according to fleshly wants will lead to nothing but bondage. Taylor Swift, having one hundred ninety-six million followers on just one of her multiple social media platforms, has this as her public bio: "Happy, Free, Confused and Lonely all at the same time." By the world's standards, with millions of dollars and millions of followers, she is happy and free, but yet she cannot deny the blatant reality that she is still confused and lonely. Surely she must be confused by the ever worsening agenda of evil and bound by the disillusion that she could be happy and free without the absolutes and truths of God's Word.

To live in truth is to truly live free. When we fill out hearts and minds with the Word of God we can say as the Psalmist said, "Therefore my heart is glad, and my glory rejoiceth" (Psalm 16:9). We can cling to the words of Jesus that say, "If the Son therefore shall make you free, ye shall be free indeed" (John 8:36). When confusion sets is we can hold fast to the promise of Christ, "Peace I leave with you, my peace I give unto you: not as the world giveth, give I unto you. Let not your heart be troubled, neither let it be afraid," (John 14:27). Loneliness must loosen its grip and leave as we declare God promise to us, "I will never leave thee, nor forsake thee," (Hebrews 13:5).

Peter knew that if the saints of God saw holiness and separation from the world as nothing more than a set of ridiculous rules that they did not understand, they would quickly and easily fall into compromise and forsake to follow the way of God. Therefore, he challenged both the early church, and the twenty-first century church alike, to add to ourselves knowledge. It is just another handful of blackberries in the whole scope of godliness yet, by our faithful pursuit of understanding we are one step close to guarding ourselves against failure.

TEMPERANCE

After being elected the thirty sixth President of the United States, it has been said that Lyndon B. Johnson was overweight. One particular day became a moment of truth as his wife confronted him with a blunt, honest assertion: "You can't run the country if you can't run yourself." Giving heed to his wife's wisdom and accurate observation, President Lyndon B. Johnson lost twenty three pounds.

Writing under the anointing and inspiration of the Holy Ghost, Peter mentions yet another thing that must be added to our lives. Temperance. It is defined as moderation in one's actions, thoughts, or feelings. To be tempered is to be restrained, yet Peter was not writing about temperance in the context of being restrained by others. His use of temperance was in reference to a child of God being able to restrain themselves. Simply put, temperance is self-control.

Knowledge is clearly important, but what good is a knowledge of truth if we lack the self-control necessary to practice what we know. James wrote saying, "To him that knoweth to do good, and doeth it not, to him it is sin," (James 4:7). Self-control is an absolute essential ingredient to our relationship with God.

"A man without self-control is like a city broken into and left without walls."
—*Unknown*

Many have surmised that the foremost factor of success is self-control. Unfortunately, it is not natural to any of us. Self-control is something that we must purposely teach ourselves through much discipline and determination. In order to strengthen our self-control we must exercise self-control. The Apostle Paul often wrote about temperance in his New Testament epistles.

"Know ye not that ye are the temple of God, and that the Spirit of God dwelleth in you? If any man defile the temple of God, him shall God destroy; for the temple of God is holy, which temple ye are."
1 Corinthians 3:16-17

"I beseech you therefore, brethren, by the mercies of God, that ye present your bodies a living sacrifice, holy, acceptable unto God, which is your reasonable service. And be not conformed to this world: but be ye transformed by the renewing of your mind, that ye may prove what is that good, and acceptable, and perfect, will of God."
Romans 12:1-2

"But I keep under my body, and bring it into subjection: lest that by any means, when I have preached to others, I myself should be a castaway."
1 Corinthians 9:27

A Handful of Blackberries: Part One

"But put ye on the Lord Jesus Christ, and make not provision for the flesh, to fulfil the lusts thereof."
Romans 13:14

Self-control brings moderation to many areas of our lives but it brings abstinence to other areas. Paul admonish to the Romans summarized it best: "Make not provision for the flesh" (Romans 13:14). Do whatever you have to do in order to bring your flesh under subjection and walk in the Spirit. Sacrifice whatever you must in order to deny the lust of your flesh. Separate yourself, be it permanent or temporary, from anything that might control you and become an idol in your life. Self-control not only brings symmetry and balance, but can bring salvation. Self-control, as set forth in scripture, puts God in control. As we crucify our fleshly desires, it allows God to lead and direct our lives.

When we push away from the table and fast food and sustenance, we are taking self off the throne and yielding our lives to the leading of the Holy Ghost. We complicate it, but it's really not all that complex. In the simplicity of sacrificing a handful of meat or bread, we are gaining a handful of temperance that is added to our lives and brings strength to our spirituality. In this present culture we need not only push away the plate, but also the many forms of pleasurable entertainment and media that are so readily available. It would do us good to log out of our social media apps and put away our favorite form of entertainment for an extended period of time so that we might add temperance to our lives and thus draw closer to the Lord.

Now the significance and value of self-control in our lives

is evident. Temperance is just another handful of blackberries. It doesn't always seem like something of great or immediate impact, but slowly we are filled up with Godly character and the ability to control and temper our sinful nature. With a handful of this and a handful of that, the child of God becomes full of faith, virtue, knowledge and temperance. With the fruit abiding in us makes life sweeter than any handful or bucketful of blackberries.

CHAPTER EIGHT

a handful
of blackberries
part two

Fear. I felt fear. During the unforgettable worldwide pandemic of 2020 that shut down our society, my husband and I looked at our calendar and it had been wiped clean. The cancellation of services and revivals had come in one after another until the foreseeable future became utterly uncertain. Being full-time evangelists, our source of income and livelihood stems from our ability to travel and minister in churches across the country. As everyone struggled to wrap their minds around what was happening and endeavor to process the impact that this pandemic would have on their families, we, too, had a lot of questions. Rather than moving on to the next town and preaching the next revival, our RV sat in Daisetta, Texas. With nowhere to go sing, no scheduled commitments to fulfill, and no roads to travel, we suddenly had more time on our hands than we knew what to do with. Actually, my introverted husband quickly adjusted and enjoyed the downtime. He logically accepted the situation for what it was and took full advantage of the opportunity to unwind and delight in a laid back relaxing lifestyle. He quickly ordered a leather-crafting, beginners toolkit and learned a new trade. Within a week or so, he was crafting hand-stitched masterpieces and loving every minute of it. I, on the other hand, had determined to personally find a way to solve the world problems so that life could be restored to its normal state and we could get back on the road again. The lack of travel, excitement, adventure, and new surroundings was more than I could stand. I was desperate to get back to the way things were supposed to be! My only saving grace was that we were parked on one of my aunt and uncle's bee keeping properties, so there was always a relative around to hang out with, and if nothing else, we had the option to suit up and visit the honeybees in the bee yards. Besides getting stung on my neck one day, it was a delightful experience, yet it wasn't our normal lifestyle that I so desperately craved.

Not only was I stir-crazy, I was fearful. It would've been nice to enjoy the season like Jeremy had, but I was too busy worrying about things like: "What if we never travel again? What if churches never get to gather again? What if we never get to sing and preach to people again? What if we never see friends and family again?" I know it sounds dramatic, but the fear was real. I never do well just sitting around, so you can only imagine my state of mind. Glumly sitting on our couch, my mind bounced around at an exceedingly great speed only to end up in discouraging and distorted places. I wanted to have purpose. I wanted to do big things. I wanted excitement and adventure. I wanted to meet new people. I wanted to minister to someone with a soul and the ability to smile back at me. Cameras can't do that! Clouded by the devilish disillusion of fear, I could see none of those things in our future.

Now, the words I had spoken in testimony on dozens of platforms around the United States echoed in my mind: "It isn't the travel and adventures that fill my heart with joy, it is Jesus alone!" How many times had I said those words with sincere emotion flooding my face, yet now I struggled to live them out. It is easy to shout faith filled claims on the mountaintop when sacrifice was the furthest thing from my mind, but now all I could see were the mountains of change that we were all being forced to make. My claims were no longer filled with faith, they were fettered by fear. I felt alone, and therefore fear made a playground of my mind. As I sat there and entertained the wrong voices which shouted their doom and gloom, I looked up at a wood sign hanging prominently on our motorhome wall, just to the right of my kitchen sink. It had been given to me by a pastor's wife who I greatly admire. It read: "Let your Faith be Bigger than Your Fears."

Although I had hung the sign and read it many times, that statement brought revelation to my mind. That was all it took to negate the lying voices I had given my ear, for it dawned on me, "faith is a choice!" Why do we let our circumstances choose the approach we take? Why do we let the uncertainties of life determine whether we live in faltering fear or freeing faith? Fear is belittling. Fear is haunting. What we fail to remember is that fear contradicts everything we know to be true.

"You gain strength, courage and confidence by every experience in which you really stop to look fear in the face. You are able to say to yourself, 'I have lived through this horror. I can take the next thing that comes along.'"
—*Eleanor Roosevelt*

Immediately I changed my outlook. I felt like Jonathan Helser must have felt when he said in song, "I'm no longer a slave to fear. I am a child of God."

I grabbed my Bible and consciously made the decision to reject fear. I choose faith over all! Over the ever-isolating reports of the media, over every lie of the enemy, over the despairing effects of negative voices, I choose faith! It was much more than choosing faith over fear, I chose faith over all. That day I chose faith over the lie that told me the church would never have revival again. I chose faith over the deception that says there is no victory in God when it seems that darkness prevails. With an opened Bible in my lap I began to declare the Word of God out loud. Knowing that the enemy thrives in disillusion and confusion, I began to combat every lie with truth. Every Scripture and promise of God that I hurled into the atmosphere of our home brought down each stronghold that fear had established. The dark cloud lifted in my mind as I intentionally decided to choose faith over all.

As I told the Lord that "I choose faith," a melody suddenly came to my mind. I began to hum what I was hearing in my head and accompany it with the declaration of my heart.

"I choose faith over all, I hold to the truth, and I won't look back. My heart will believe even things yet unseen and I won't look back."

Almost a year later, that melody and those words would come alive in a Nashville studio, but for the moment they were for none but me. I didn't know if it would ever be heard or become the anthem of others, but it was my anthem. I soon coupled my words with the Word of Scripture and sang 2

Timothy 1:7 out loud, "For God hath not given us the spirit of fear, but of power, love, and a sound mind."

The enemy had succeeded in convincing me that God had forsaken us and our promised future had faded away, but faith convinced me all the more that God had not changed, and His hands were not tied. Once I conquered the crippling fear that had consumed my mind and spirit, I began to notice that God was miraculously supplying our every need. Pastors from all over the country, some that we knew and others that we didn't, were contacting us asking that we minister to their churches via video. There were others who just sent offerings and expressed that they felt led to be a blessing to us during those uncertain days. It really blew my mind when Jeremy told me of several people, who are not ministers or even faithful church goers, sending us donations to offset our living expenses. I guess I shouldn't have been, but I was amazed! God was providing our needs, and I had failed to see it until I conquered fear and chose to live in faith.

During those weeks and months in which society was shut down, we were blessed to minister in church parking lots. We sang and preached to video cameras in empty sanctuaries. It was weird and uncomfortable, but we saw the glory of God. He never hid himself from us nor did He withhold anything from our hand.

"Consider the lilies of the field, how they grow; they toil not, neither do they spin: And yet I say unto you, That even Solomon in all his glory was not arrayed like one of these. Wherefore, if God so clothe the grass of the field, which to day is, and to morrow is cast into the oven, shall he not much more clothe you, O ye of little

faith? Therefore take no thought, saying, What shall we eat? or, What shall we drink? or, Wherewithal shall we be clothed? (For after all these things do the Gentiles seek:) for your heavenly Father knoweth that ye have need of all these things. But seek ye first the kingdom of God, and his righteousness; and all these things shall be added unto you."
Matthew 6:28-33

Many nights during that season I would read my Bible until my eyes grew heavy with sleep. My renewed choice of faith produced a fresh hunger for the Word of God. I'm ashamed to admit it, but it's true: it took a global pandemic and an empty calendar to teach me how to choose faith and trust the Lord in a deeper way. Now I know that it sometimes takes an absence of plenty in order for us to seek out the source of our strength and joy.

After about six weeks without travel, Jeremy and I finally were able to pack up the RV and hit the road again. Churches were opening back up in Oklahoma, and we jumped at the opportunity to step back into our calling and see revival take place. Nevertheless, during those weeks of waiting, I learned the importance of adding patience to my faith.

PATIENCE

"Rest in the LORD, and wait patiently for him:" Psalm 37:7

Patience is more than a trait, it is a way of living. To trust in the Lord is to wait upon Him; therefore every believer must add to themselves patience. Without it we will fail to remain faithful and steadfast in those seasons when it seems as though God has forsaken us. Anyone who has ever walked through one of those seasons, you know what I am talking about. Those who have not yet experienced the waiting, it will surely come. How easy it is to become impatient in the waiting, to be tempted to take control of our own destinies. Even from Scripture we could compile a long list of people who learned the lesson of patience the hard way. Leading that list is Abraham and Sarah, who eventually doubted that God would indeed fulfill His promise of giving them a son. Their impatience with God and wavering faith in His word led Sarah to believe that Abraham should marry her maid Hagar and, by her, father the son through whom God said all the nations of the earth would be blessed. Everything seemed to go according to their plan until Sarah conceived at the age of ninety years old. They had grown impatient, yet God remained faithful and true to His Word. You and I are prone to make that same mistake but also have the privilege to learn from Abraham and Sarah's impatient and endeavor to get right what they got wrong. We must develop patience that is not swayed by the seeming inactivity of God around us. When time has passed and God has yet to come through like He promised, we must be content to wait until His Word is fulfilled. We must posses patience that is undergirded by loyalty and commitment. Each of us must decide within ourselves that we will hold to His unchanging hand and, even in the waiting, remain loyal to Him. When we have prayed and fasted for the healing of our bodies and nothing happens, we must remain loyal in our faith. When we have believed the promises of

God yet have seen no results, we must remain unwavering in our commitment to trust the Lord until the time of fulfillment comes. When we have labored and toiled in the harvest without yielding any return, we must even then exercise patience and know that God will give the increase as He promised. Waiting isn't always easy, but it's always worth it.

> *"Be joyful in hope, patient in affliction, faithful in prayer."*
> *Romans 12:12 (NIV)*

Waiting can often feel like a wilderness through which we must wander, but there are things we can do that will sustain us in the waiting. First of all, keep hope alive in your heart! Don't let doubt or unbelief convince you that the ship has sailed or the time of fulfillment has come and gone. There is no doubt our hope may take a hit at times, but we must keep hope alive. As long as there is hope, there can be joy in our hearts.

Secondly, Paul admonished the Romans to be patient in affliction. God often leads us through certain seasons and guides us through dark places for the purpose of teaching our hearts, strengthening our spirits, and developing our faith. I once heard a preacher say, "What you suffer through, you gain dominion over." Affliction, pain, suffering, and trouble are never easy to endure, yet we must decide to patiently wait upon the Lord and trust that He will use this present suffering for our good.

Thirdly, we must never fail to be faithful in prayer. One will never succeed in patience unless he first succeeds in faithfulness of prayer. Those holy moments of sweet communion with God are when we can bare our soul before Him and, in return, receive strength for the day. I've often wondered, "How do people make it through life without prayer?" When I am frustrated, prayer renews my faith. When I am lonely, prayer reveals that I am surrounded by the Almighty. When I am weak, prayer gives me strength. When I am ready to give up, prayer urges me onward.

Peter was certainly right. Without a handful of patience every day, we are sure to fall.

"But they that wait upon the LORD shall renew their strength; they shall mount up with wings as eagles; they shall run, and not be weary; and they shall walk, and not faint."
Isaiah 40:31

GODLINESS

"O worship the LORD in the beauty of holiness: fear before him, all the earth."
Psalm 96:9

I once read of a mother who visited her son's college dorm room. Stepping through the doorway, she was disappointed to see that the walls were covered with suggestive immoral pictures. Her heart broke, but she said nothing. After returning home, she mailed her son a package. The boy anxiously opened the box and found a beautifully framed portrait of Christ. To please his mother, he proudly hung that picture on the wall above his desk. After hanging there for only a few hours, something began to change in that young man's heart. Before bed, he removed the suggestive picture that hung closest to the face of Christ. The next day another picture was taken down and thrown into the trashcan. Day after day the pictures began to disappear from the walls until only one remained, the portrait of Jesus Christ (Encyclopedia of Illustrations #5065).

> *"...dearly beloved, let us cleanse ourselves from all filthiness of the flesh and spirit, perfecting holiness in the fear of God."*
> *2 Corinthians 7:1*

Contrary to the popular opinion of our culture, godliness is beautiful. Scripture speaks of holiness in such high regard that the writer of Hebrews clearly stated that without it "no man shall see the Lord." (Hebrews 12:14) Therefore, not only are godliness and holiness beautiful, they are essential.

> *"You shall be holy, for I am holy."*
> *Leviticus 11:45*

The Lord commanded this of the children of Israel whom He delivered out of bondage in Egypt and from the hand of Pharaoh. When the Apostle Peter was writing his first new testament epistle, he quickly launched into the subject of godliness. Along with many of his own words which were inspired of the Holy Ghost, Peter reached back into the ancient text of the law and referenced the words of God given to Israel. Just as holiness had been required of the Hebrew nation, Peter declared that it was still required of the New

Testament church also. There have been many to come along in the twenty-first century and claim that holiness is no longer necessary or important. They say that holiness is nothing more than an unrealistic expectation that is outdated and antiquated, no longer relevant to reach this current culture. Simply put, they could not be more wrong. We have been called unto holiness and godliness.

"I beseech you therefore, brethren, by the mercies of God, that ye present your bodies a living sacrifice, holy, acceptable unto God, which is your reasonable service."
Romans 12:1

Holiness is still what pleases God. Hypocrisy by some has driven many to hate the way of holiness, but we cannot let the actions of others keep us from living lives that are acceptable and pleasing unto the Lord. The bottom line of all that we do in an effort to be holy is this: "I want to please the Lord." The modesty of my dress, the words of my mouth, the content of character, and the path that I walk are to be a reflection of the God whom I serve.

"Holiness is the habit of being of one mind with God, according as we find His mind described in Scripture. It is the habit of agreeing in God's judgment, hating what He hates, loving what He loves, and measuring everything in this world by the standard of His Word."
— J. C. Ryle

We can be easily tempted to wonder, "Do these actions of holiness really matter? Is it really necessary that I separate myself from sin and the things of this world?" To be sure, it matters. They may at times seem simple and mundane, but they are but another handful of blackberries. Don't give up but keep being godly! With every handful of holiness, you become a little more like Him.

BROTHERLY KINDNESS

One of Aesop's fables is the tale of an old man with several sons who were always falling out with one another. He had often exhorted them to live together in harmony, but it was always to no avail. One day he called them together and challenged each one of his sons to break a bundle of sticks that he had tied tightly together. Each one of them endeavored to do what the brother before him couldn't do, yet none of them could break the bundle of sticks. After everyone had taken their turn, the father cut the cord and told his sons to break each stick separately. That was done with the greatest ease. "See, my sons," the old man said "the power of unity!" When we are bound together by brotherly love, we can defy almost every mortal danger, but divided we will fall prey to every enemy.

> *"…a threefold cord is not quickly broken"*
> *Ecclesiastes 4:12*

No wonder Jesus commanded us to "love thy neighbour as thyself" (Matthew 22:39) That is not to say we will never disagree or differ from those around us, but we must never fail to demonstrate love. Being so greatly loved by God, we therefore have a responsibility to love others as we have been loved. We need one another, therefore we cannot be divided by differences or demographics.

> *"If a man say, I love God, and hateth his brother, he is a liar: for he that loveth not his brother whom he hath seen, how can he love God whom he hath not seen?"*
> 1 John 4:20

The premium that God has placed upon brotherly kindness is high and directly related to the validity of our love toward Him. If we hate our brother, God does not delight in the worship we bring or the sacrifice we offer unto Him, however sincere we are. From His perspective, our love for Him is contingent upon our love for fellow man.

Jesus made this concept clear to his disciples on the night before His crucifixion. At the conclusion of their supper Jesus arose from the table, laid aside His outer garments, tied a towel around His waist, and spoke words of instruction unto His closest followers. John 13:34 "A new commandment I give to you, that you love one another: just as I have loved you, you also are to love one another." Thus, sacrifice without obedience is no great thing.

> *"Does the Lord delight in burnt offerings and sacrifices as much as in obeying the Lord? To obey is better than sacrifice and to heed is better than the fat of rams."*
> 1 Samuel 15:22

A Handful of Blackberries: Part Two

In Matthew 5:23-24, God tells the people in the Sermon on the Mount, "Therefore, if you are offering your gift at the altar and there remember that your brother or sister has something against you, leave your gift there in front of the altar. First go and be reconciled to them; then come and offer your gift."

God is the very definition of love, therefore to be His, is to be known for our love for one another.

"Anyone who does not love does not know God, because God is love."
1 John 4:8 (ESV)

We become who we spend our time with, thus being a child of God, surely love will become a part of us. "Beloved, let us love one another, for love is from God, and whoever loves has been born of God and knows God" (1 John 4:7 ESV).

"By this all people will know that you are my disciples, if you have love for one another."
John 13:35

We cannot have true love for this world without first loving our brother. Isn't it funny how we as humans can be most critical on the ones closest to us? We can be friendly to a suspicious stranger in the grocery store, only to turn around and take out the frustrations we bare on our loved ones. God commands us and has it plainly put in His word, we must love our brother before we can love this world. This is so important to the Lord, yet our pride, personality conflicts, and frustrations wants to negate the truth that to be

166

biblical is to love our brother as ourselves. It is only with love like that, the world sees how pure our love can be for them. They see that to be a part of what we have is safe and desirable indeed! It is a delight to the devil to sow discord among the brethren, for surely then, we do not look like Christ's disciples.

Our loving words to a lost soul will fail and sound like obnoxious symbols in their ears when they see the hypocrisy and inconsistencies with the ones closest to us. To the lost soul, why would they want to become a brother and sister of us, when we treat a brother and sister with disdain? Without love, our words are cheap and detrimental. But with brotherly love, there is no fear! Love is forever more of God.

"Having purified your souls by your obedience to the truth for a sincere brotherly love, clove one another earnestly from a pure heart"
1 Peter 1:22 (ESV)

To love and prefer our brother or sister means there may be times we could do something, yet it would be a hindrance to them or even their demise, so we choose not to. Paul exemplifies this selfless love when he wrote in 1 Corinthians 8:13 (NIV), "Therefore, if what I eat causes my brother or sister to fall into sin, I will never eat meat again, so that I will not cause them to fall."

It seems small, choosing not do certain things to help my brother or my sister. It is a mere handful of berries in the whole scope of life. But this one, this one is even more important than our own salvation, this one is about someone else's salvation, too.

167

A Handful of Blackberries: Part Two

LOVE

Things are precious often because of their relationship. We are precious to God for we are His children. He first loves us, therefore we love Him. He has created us in His image, therefore love is obtainable to all. At times, our love may be covered up with layers of brutal bitterness, hindering hurt, and jilting jealousy. Yet when those layers are peeled back, we find exposed in every soul the ability to love, when in close proximity to Jesus. Love is still the strongest force. Martin Luther King Jr said it well, "I have decided to stick with love. Hate is too great a burden to bear." Even more than sticking with it, we are all called and commanded to it. In Matthew 22:36-39 when Jesus was asked a question on the greatest of commandments, we find the greatest were indeed the ones which contained love. "Teacher, which is the greatest commandment in the Law?"Jesus replied: "'Love the Lord your God with all your heart and with all your soul and with all your mind.' This is the first and greatest commandment. And the second is like it: 'Love your neighbor as yourself." (NIV)

Without love, at best we are a clanging symbol. At worst and more realistic, we are lost for eternity.

The anointed Paul pens the words with eloquence, understanding, and true definition of love. Far be it for me to compete with my own definition, when these words, straight from the Word of God, are what we must read and dwell upon.

"If I speak in the tongues of men or of angels, but do not have love, I am only a resounding gong or a clanging cymbal. If I

have the gift of prophecy and can fathom all mysteries and all knowledge, and if I have a faith that can move mountains, but do not have love, I am nothing. If I give all I possess to the poor and give over my body to hardship that I may boast, but do not have love, I gain nothing. Love is patient, love is kind. It does not envy, it does not boast, it is not proud. It does not dishonor others, it is not self-seeking, it is not easily angered, it keeps no record of wrongs. Love does not delight in evil but rejoices with the truth. It always protects, always trusts, always hopes, always perseveres. Love never fails. But where there are prophecies, they will cease; where there are tongues, they will be stilled; where there is knowledge, it will pass away. For we know in part and we prophesy in part, but when completeness comes, what is in part disappears. When I was a child, I talked like a child, I thought like a child, I reasoned like a child. When I became a man, I put the ways of childhood behind me. For now we see only a reflection as in a mirror; then we shall see face to face. Now I know in part; then I shall know fully, even as I am fully known. And now these three remain: faith, hope and love. But the greatest of these is love."
1 Corinthians 13 (NIV)

Oh, how often have I fallen short on such love! Do you see your own reflection woven within the definition of love, or find yourself falling short within the first paragraph? Do not be discouraged, there is much hope. Have faith! To love more means to draw closer to the One Who is Love. Love never fails. Jesus never fails.

A Handful of Blackberries: Part Two

OUR OVERFLOWING CUP

Somehow, with each handful added, we step back and see the overflowing bucket of blackberries and can only exclaim, "... my cup runneth over. Surely goodness and mercy shall follow me all the days of my life: and I will dwell in the house of the LORD for ever" (Psalm 23:5-6).

How could there be room for our demise when we are already full? Nothing could fit inside of us to make us fall; our cup overflows. Following these God-given verses, our life will produce many things more beautiful than a pan of blackberry brownies or homemade jams. The goodness and beauty of a life thriving in Jesus goes beyond any delightful dessert, although sweet indeed it is living for Jesus. He has held me every day I have lived, and although I could never claim to know what tomorrow holds, I do know who holds my tomorrow. I do not know the road God will call my husband and me on next, but I choose to trust the Master's Hand.

Oh, can't you see, have I not convinced you that every word written in this book is to remind us God alone is worthy of our faith! It is He who sets up kings and takes them down, it is He alone who hung the stars in the sky, and it is He who breathes life into our lungs. He all by Himself is the only one proven faithful and true throughout time. Every story and experience I have shared is all for one purpose, to let an anthem arise within each one of us, "I choose Faith over All."

"I choose faith over all, I hold to the truth, and I won't look back.
My heart will believe even things yet unseen, and I won't give up.
For God hath not given a spirit of fear, but of power, love, and
a sound mind.
I choose Faith over all, I hold to the truth, and I won't look back.
My heart will believe even things yet unseen, and I won't give up."